For Rev. Isabelle —

Many Blessings and Peace!

Michael Firth

*Psychic Integrity*

# Psychic Integrity

*Ethics and Morals of Modern-Day Mystics*

*Melissa Leath*

*Notice*: **UltraSense(TM)** and its specific meaning used in this text is trademarked by Melissa Leath (2003), and may not be used in any fashion without express permission of the author, except by a reviewer who may quote brief passages in a review.

Words that may need more definition to the reader will appear in the book in **bold type**. This is a clue to look for more explanation in the back of the book under **Glossary.**

*The Go-Between: Bridging the Gap* (2003, out-of-print) by Melissa Leath is the forerunner for *Psychic Integrity.* Many ideas and concepts shared here originated in *The Go-Between.* With the need for integrity so great, and a better understanding of the psychic/medium process, Leath completely expanded the original book to this full reveal.

ISBN 0-9760749-5-8

Additional copies of this book may be ordered. Group orders invited. Call for details.

937-323-5346
Off the Beaten Path Intuitive Arts
Email: psychicintegrity@gmail.com
Website: www.PsychicIntegrity.com

Printed in the United States of America by CreateSpace

# Table of Contents

# Acknowledgements

I have such gratitude to the Universal Creator for bringing this book into existence. Without the experiences and teachings over my lifetime, I could not share this information.

My husband Charles has always been my source of strength and encouragement, constantly pushing me forward. With his strength I completed the book I believe is essential at this time.

I'd like to thank Sharon Smythe for her friendship and being co-teacher with me over the past three years. Teaching our Psychic and Spiritual Awakening Classes encouraged me with the idea of teaching integrity.

I'm very grateful to Denise and George Tucker who helped me form my ideas into positive words of inspiration.

Special thanks to Luan Heit, my editor, who helped me take those words and present them in a proper way.

Many blessings to them all.

# Introduction to
# *Psychic Integrity*

# Introduction

Do the words *moral, integrity* and *psychic* sound like a strange combination? They go together like peanut butter and jelly. The blending of these words is the full potential of all intuitive people.

Over the years, the word *psychic* developed an infamous reputation. It is the main reason I never used the word as a description of what I did. Psychics have been stereotyped as scam artists, fortune-tellers, or dishonest readers.

Early in my teachings of spiritualism, I recognized the problem and how the general public saw what I do. I decided to use the word **intuitive** instead of the word **psychic.**

To validate the decision, when I started giving readings to the public (as opposed to only within the church setting), my husband Charles, a reflexologist, and I set up a booth at a local flea market. It was a way of advertising what we do to the community.

My sign said, *Intuitive Readings*. After several days, I wasn't getting much attention with passers-by. Charles suggested I change the sign to *Psychic Readings*. He said no one really knew what intuitive meant, but would understand the word psychic.

So, I changed the sign.

That same afternoon, an older couple was talking to Charles about reflexology. He invited them into our booth. The wife saw me and my sign and said, "No! I won't go in there. Not with that *psychic* in there."

This brought to my attention just how strongly people feel about psychics.

The sign was destroyed.

However, society is changing their perception of psychics. A Gallup Poll was conducted for the Committee for the Scientific Investigation of Claims of the Paranormal in 2005.

During the poll, out of 1002 participants 18 years of age and older, 73% believed in some kind of paranormal event. Some of the paranormal beliefs were:

- ESP (Extra Sensory Perception)-41%
- Haunted Houses-37%
- Ghosts-32%
- Telepathy-31%
- Clairvoyance-26%
- Astrology-25%
- Communication with the Dead-21%
- Reincarnation-20%
- Channeling Spirit Entities-9%.

Today, because new television programming includes psychic and paranormal events, the opportunities for recognition are much greater.

Sharing paranormal activities in the media has opened the profession to many people who were not aware of it before. More individuals than ever recognize they have psychic abilities. Many of them are making very nice careers in this field. Some are truly powerful psychics and mediums.

Even though there are honest, gifted readers, the public still generally recognizes the dishonest ones as the norm.

Fortunately there are many ways to determine whether psychics are ethical and have high integrity. This is the main focus of *Psychic Integrity*.

There are scam artists who fraudulently present themselves as psychics. They continue to cloak themselves with sensational bits of information for their clients, without giving substance to the message. Other readers can recognize them immediately.

The unsuspecting public is still uninformed and unaware of the gray areas of readings. They do not understand the dynamics of communicating with the spirits of deceased loved ones. Often they fall for deceptions in their ignorance and heartfelt pain.

A most logical way to find someone reputable would be to ask friends with an interest in psychics who they recommend. The best regulation of the psychic industry is word of mouth information.

There are no definitive guidelines to measure abilities; no professional policies to refer to; and no established governing body to report problem psychics. This makes it difficult for potential clients to have any kind of yardstick for knowing where to look and what to look for.

My hope is this book becomes the guideline for all psychics and a reference for those who are looking to find a reader of integrity.

With this book, I created a standard to strive for to be used by psychic and intuitive readers of all kinds. It is a textbook for all of my **intuitive, clairvoyant** and **medium** unfoldment students. It is required reading for certification in my courses, as part of the curriculum.

My greatest wish is for this to be used as a definitive guide for all who are (or will be) reading for clients in any way---whether it be psychic, mediumship, **tarot, numerology, psychometry, astrology, channeling,** etc.

But more, I present it as a way for potential clients to discern the appropriate reader for them selves and understand the study, training and practice needed to use the gift appropriately.

The entire work with psychic and spirit energy is to be considered a sacred matter. I believe it to be a tool of spirituality. This is not to be confused with religion, per se. Although many religions embrace communication with spirit energies and the Higher Self, I don't presume to say it is necessary to be of any particular religious faith.

However, since I do see it as a higher calling, and connected with Creator Source, I feel it is necessary to invite or ask for the highest vibrations and spirit beings possible to be associated with activities such as psychic readings.

All readers should begin their work with a special protective affirmation, ritual or prayer. This keeps both the client and the reader protected.

To support my thoughts of sacred work here, let me include just a few mediums from holy texts.

The letter from Paul to the Corinthians in the Bible, Chapter 2:4, "and my speech and my preaching was not with enticing words of man's wisdom, but in demonstration of the spirit and the power." This plainly statements his speech was channeled information brought through him through spirit inspiration.

King Saul visited the Witch of Endor. He was worried about Israel being threatened by the Philistines. He asked her to bring up the spirit of the prophet Samuel.

Jesus was perhaps the most well known and documented medium in the Bible. He was able to heal the sick, create material manifestation (change water into wine), feed a crowd of people with only a few loaves and fishes, walk on water, and calm the raging sea. This is evidence of physical mediumship.

John 4: 16-19, "The woman saith unto him, Sir, give me this water, that I thirst not, neither come hither to draw. Jesus saith unto her, Go, call thy husband, and come hither. The woman answered and said I have no husband. Jesus said unto her, Thou hast well said, I have no husband: For thou hast had five husbands; and he whom thou now hast is not thy husband; in that sadist thou truly. The woman saith unto him, Sir, I perceive that thou art a prophet."

Most of us are already conscious of the spirit realm when we are asleep or in a quiet state of reverie. The term **metaphysical** actually means beyond the physical. It is used to recognize we are more than physical beings. We also have mind and spirit. Metaphysics relates to all things, including physical. It deals with a holistic approach to life and living, and what may be unrecognized by our physicality.

When thinking metaphysically, we are thinking outside the box of society. We allow the possibility of other things not yet considered.

I prefer to walk in faith, not by what I must see. Not all things of this world can be touched or seen physically. But we know them to be real, such as love for your child, patriotism, the way you feel when you smell new-mowed grass. These things exist but cannot be seen physically.

I lived most of my life by faith. I never felt like I had to prove anything to anyone. When I receive information through the spirit I don't need outside proof.

There are many researchers and scientists who would love to be able to dissect the spiritual dimension to see what there is to see. I don't have to hold it in my hand to know it is real. But many people do.

This is the difference between people that makes us individual. I ask you to take things as they are. Don't always look for proof. There are many things you know without someone telling you, without reading it in a book, or seeing it on television.

No scientist can research your feelings and tell you, for instance, that you are lonely. It is something you just know.

If you feel broken-hearted because your husband just passed away, no surgeon can operate on you, look at your heart and see the break. Yet, it is there.

Going one step further, being told by a psychic reader you are lonely or heart broken is one thing. That could be the sensational part of the reading.

Is it the important thing: That you are lonely? After all, you already knew it. Isn't it more important to receive information to help you in your loneliness? Perhaps there is an underlying reason you are lonely. It could be self-esteem or you are different than the others around you.

Perhaps it can spur you into action. Does it help to tell you about your loneliness? Or would it be better to work towards the resolve of the situation?

This is where I feel spirituality comes into play. Don't we have a duty to always give the best and highest information possible to help our client? To dazzle someone is only good for the moment. Fireworks don't last.

Of course, fireworks will get attention. After the client is paying attention, give them what their soul is looking for.

For instance: We have soul purpose in the world. Maybe the person in question is lonely because she has steered off her path so far, the soul needs to shake her up a little.

Recognizing the spirit in others is your mission. Understand what her soul is trying to tell her, but was not paying attention to. Then assist your client back to wholeness.

The information in *Psychic Integrity* is given to you for your knowledge in understanding how to recognize positive and ethical behavior in psychic readers and mediums. It is for anyone who works with the public in an intuitive manner.

In this book, I write about many of my own experiences and information I've learned while working with clients. That's the best way I can share my information.

I cover everything from how to find a good reader that matches your personality, to recognizing a reader of high integrity. It includes all the study, knowledge and experience that go into becoming a professional reader.

# Chapter One

*Basic Ethical Principles*

# Basic Ethical Principles

*What are Ethics?*

The concept of ethics is generally described as professional standards of conduct; uprightness and honor: being fair. Ethics are derived from social commonalities. They come as a result of what is deemed as usual or "the customary response".

Many psychic readers think of ethical behavior as something such as: I will charge you a fair price; I will not share your information with anyone; I will refer you to a professional who may assist you, such as lawyer, financial expert or psychologist.

I feel ethics start (or should start) many years before the person begins working with clients as a reader. Much of it comes as part of your upbringing and the way your parents or families teach you about life and respect. It has to do with your integrity.

The integrity needed for readers comes as they are learning to use their psychic gifts. Many are born with these gifts, but may not instantly know how to relate the information to the client. They may not know about the higher and lower levels of entities sending the information.

It could very well be coming from a low vibration wanting to trick them or just play around. So discernment of sources is very important.

This all comes with study, practice under mentorship, and trial and error. That is why I have included a whole section on **unfoldment**. Unfoldment means allowing your gift to evolve or grow. Some call it unfoldment, because it is unfolding a spiritual gift already existing, allowing it to expand and become stronger. This is the perfect way to understand what the gift is all about, how it works and experience it in the long term. Unfoldment is usually exclusive to a circle of potential mediums and taking the time for the gifts to mature.

Many use the word development, which means to bring about or produce. It gives the thought of purposefully taking classes and being taught through experience. Development seems to be more aggressive in the approach.

I may use the words interchangeably but do realize they are different. The process of maturing the ability is what brings the reader into high integrity and knowing how to present the information coming through them in an honest, ethical and reliable manner.

## Ethical Statements

Many psychics consider offering advice or dealing with information of a personal nature as a business, and have a code of ethics to govern that business or protect themselves and the interest of their clients.

This would, of course include the professional psychic. The code of ethics is something felt as being important to make known to the general public.

I've researched many materials of psychic readers and psychic organizations and have come up with a composite of ethical statements they have listed.

Below is a sample of what many professional psychics make available to their clients:

*I Promise to---*

- Always serve the best interest of my clients, and conduct my professional activities without intentionally causing harm.

- Treat all my clients with respect regardless of origin, race, religion, gender, age or sexual preference.

- Honestly present my qualifications, including educational credentials and levels of certification.

- Keep confidential the names of clients and information shared or discussed during readings.

- Recommend consultation with a licensed professional for advice of a legal, financial, medical or psychological nature I am not qualified to provide.

- Respect my client's right to end their reading at any time.

These are statements I agree with. They are definitely necessary for anyone in business on a personal level. I want to take it a step further.

Integrity is what should be defining ethical behavior. The issue is not how you work with the general public.

It is how you live your life, how you are trained, how you learn, how you practice your abilities: being the best you can be for your client.

Many readers also state their readings are for entertainment purposes only. Although many of the readings I do are humorous and light hearted, I do not consider them entertainment. This gives the feel of a three-ring circus.

Psychic work is a much higher calling than entertainment. I take it very seriously, and intend it to be of value to my client. It should be an aid in looking to the future, in decision-making and understanding past or present circumstances.

I understand some psychics use the words "for entertainment purposes" to protect themselves from the general public who may unscrupulously accuse them of deceit or fortune-telling. For those psychics I suggest they pursue a counselor's license or minister's license.

Pursuing further education would fully complete their dedication to assisting other's with their life problems. It would be the most logical direction for anyone who works with the public in a caring and dedicated manner. Each person is encouraged to look into his/her local and state government laws for guidance in this area.

## *Attitude of Responsibility*

As a young child, you display an attitude of dependence; and rightfully so. All the things you learn require acceptance: Believing that your parents, older siblings and people of authority are right.

You trust and accept. As you grow older and become a teenager, you instinctively change your attitude to one of independence.

It can be difficult to know when to trust, when to show your knowledge, or lack of it. This display of independence, or challenge of authority, can often get you in trouble.

This change of attitude continues until you are able to know when it is all right to challenge and when it is expected to be dependent. By the time you become adult, you have gained in knowledge, and the ability to show proper respect for those of greater knowledge. You know when to trust in your own abilities, and when to seek help and guidance.

Growing in spirituality and psychic abilities requires the same learning methods as growing from childhood, to the teen years and on to adulthood. By the time you have grown to adulthood (spiritually speaking) you have learned how to trust in your own abilities.

Responsibility comes through knowledge. Being spiritually adult gives you great responsibility. Psychic readers are responsible for the information they share with their clients. They are required to be educated enough and adult enough in their spirituality, to be a responsible source of information and service.

There is no excuse for wrong action. You aren't the child you used to be. You have been given wisdom; you must use it correctly. Now is the time to adopt the attitude of responsibility.

By your attitude, you assume a position. An attitude of responsibility is to assume you are capable of adult action. As you grow in spirituality and develop your intuition and psychic ability, you realize the seriousness of the gift. It is always to be used in love and to uplift everyone you are connected with.

*SIDE COMMENT~*
*Becoming spiritually adult requires a giant leap of faith. Along with that faith is the realization you are capable of making good, sound decisions. Having a responsible attitude is to know you are ready for spirit to move you in the right decisions*

If asked to provide information, always reach for and only allow the most highly evolved spirits to assist you. Those working with spirit guidance do not always receive information. Sometimes the connection is weak, or nonexistent. Honor that. If you recognize it happening, be truthful about it. Do not make up answers not there.

You are the only one who can control your integrity. There is honor in every tradition, and this age-old tradition is no exception.

Those who have come for counsel will appreciate and respect the truthful spiritual reader. Simply state you are not receiving anything. When the time is right, the answer will be there. It cannot be forced.

## Unethical Soliciting

During the time I sat in unfoldment class many years ago, I began to notice something while standing in line at the grocery store one day. I was minding my own business---or so I thought.

I realized the woman standing in front of me had a horrid fight with her husband. She stormed out of the house and ended up at the grocery.

I was astonished at the strong feeling coming from her. Sympathy came into my heart for her. I felt so badly for her, but didn't know what to do. What could I say to help her?

All of a sudden, I realized I was invading her private space! I was picking up information in her vibrations without her knowledge or permission.  I was in the middle of her life drama. It was not a good feeling

Delving into other's energy fields without permission was never addressed or explained in the teachings I received.

While at church, I watched other advanced mediums. One or two were always very popular, because they were always tuned in, psychically.

Being tuned in means they were always receiving information about people and situations. If someone came by them to say hello, the psychic would dig into that individual's personal business, psychically. You could always get information from these psychics. They heard spirit all the time.

"Your guides are telling me..." "The angels don't want you to...." The medium was always in the middle of everyone's business. It felt like an invasion of privacy.

The only time a spirit medium should be in someone's vibration is after the person or client asked, or permission is given.

If you know someone like that, you may notice how he or she tries to tune in to things all the time, or while around someone they don't know very well. When a medium is dealing in the spirit vibration all the time, they are not dealing in the physical dimension very well.

There must be a happy medium (forgive the pun!) between the spiritual and physical dimensions. After constant contact with spirit energy, she may not be able to make decisions on her own.

She has to ask spirit for even mundane advice. That could be because the medium is not confident in herself or her gifts. So she constantly has to prove herself.

## Setting Guidelines

I decided to set certain guidelines for my **spirit guides**. That is what they are for. I spoke very openly and earnestly with my wonderful group of guiding forces.

I told them I did not want to know every detail of everyone's business. While during the course of a regular day, I did not want to be bombarded with information about this person or that person.

Also, the only time I wanted to be in connection with others' vibrations was during a consultation or reading. Saying a prayer of protection and invocation would put me into a special vibration and state of universal knowledge (this is what I call being "**in spirit**").

I made sure if there was something important, concerning my safety, I could receive the correct vibrational connection. But by no means should I be left open all day long.

After a length of time, I was able to open and close my own vibrational tunnel when I wanted or needed to. To this day, I still do not nose around in others' vibrations.

Occasionally someone will ask what I'm picking up on a certain event, or person. I tell them honestly I wasn't tuned in.

I am content not treading in unsolicited territory. I believe the gift of intuition is to be used as a loving tool of counsel and confirmation. All readers working with their clients in a spiritual counseling session should be doing the same thing.

## A Matter of Excellence

Taken from John Gardner's book, "Excellence", he stresses something more than high standards. He explores several ideas I feel are worthy of mentioning here, dealing with integrity and self-development.

*Self-knowledge*: About self-knowledge he says if we falter, it is through the heart and spirit that we fail. But the discovery of talent is only one side of self-development. The other side is self-knowledge. Find time to be alone. Find yourself; know what your soul looks like.

*Motivation:* It's very easy to get caught in the rut of taking the easy way out when dealing with the integrity of living. A person who is self motivated may need to use a certain degree of sheer physical energy.

Gardner goes on to say how important it is to find your own capacity to learn, grow and overcome life's challenges. Always nourish yourself as an independent being. Honor your own values and those of others.

*Meaning, Purpose and Commitment:* There is not just one meaning or purpose to life. There are many reasons for living. Some are found early in life, some are found late. Some are highly emotional in nature, some are intellectual, some spiritual and some societal. But each reason involves a relationship of obligations and rewards.

Meaning, purpose and commitment become blended as you come across each reason for life. Many other layers of your self unfold: Who am I? Why am I here? What commitments do I have to myself and others? Excellence comes by understanding and a willingness to embrace the idea of integrity.

## Mistrust in the Trade

After looking at some of the writings found in the Harry Price Library of Magical Literature, University of London, I found a very good description as to why readers had difficulty in maintaining respect in their field.

In Old England (during the time of King Henry VIII), laws were passed providing severe punishments for fortune telling. It mainly spoke of "Egypsyans," referring to gypsies. Anyone using palmistry, fortune telling or any other "deception", as the law put it, and stayed in the area for the length of one month were known automatically as felons.

This particular law is the reason for many speculations. Groups of gypsies have long been known to use spirit powers and gifts in their work.

But I also know they are well known for being a traveling band. The Law, as written here would certainly explain why a group would have to travel and not stay put in one area. I imagine these circumstances presented themselves as a result of the law, and not the other way around.

As society continued and these laws were imposed on psychics and mediums, I feel the term "psychic" began its downward spiral into negative meaning.

It created doubt and suspicion within the land and the general public unfortunately believed the worst.

Laws against fortune telling eventually became less severe. In 1824, a law in Great Britain stated fortune-tellers and mediums may be prosecuted.

Any person pretending to tell fortunes or to deceive any of His Majesty's subjects would be called a Rogue and Vagabond. This person could be put to hard labor for up to three months.

Let's take a look at some of the early laws in the United States. There have been many attempts to discredit mediums and fortune-tellers as being fakes.

A Bill (H.R. 8989) was introduced by Sol Bloom, representative in congress from the state of New York, in 1926 that made fortune telling illegal.

It states anyone pretending to tell fortunes or using fraud to obtain payment would be considered a disorderly person and imprisoned for six months and fined $250.

The direction we have decided to pursue as assisting others in their lives has been in question for some time now. It is of utmost importance we cultivate our trade in the highest degree to ensure the reputation is clear: we are here to help, not hurt.

There needs to be more than just a standard of normal behavior; more than ethics, we need high integrity to govern our foundation. We may have to do more, than less, to balance out the damage done over the years.

# Chapter 2

## *Intuition, Psychics and Mediumship*

# Intuition, Psychics, and Mediumship

These three terms are often used to represent the same thing. Even though they are related, they mean very different things. Let's look at an example of how intuition, psychic ability and mediumship can work in the same situation:

A mother sends her child to school in the morning, as usual. A few hours later she feels as though something is wrong. She may actually shake off the feeling as being too over-protective of her child. This is an example of recognizing intuition and then being in denial of it. We do it every day. Have you ever said to yourself, "I knew that was going to happen," after denying an intuitive hit, yourself?

The feeling continues despite her efforts to engage in other activities. Soon the school nurse calls to say her child fell, injuring his knee.

These are easy vibrations for us to recognize. We are always tuned in to our family's vibrations because we are concerned about their well-being.

There are several ways the mother could have received this information:

1. Intuition is the most obvious: a subtle way of reaching into energy fields unconsciously to know information. It is so subtle that we usually explain it away. We all have this ability. It is quite often called mother's intuition or gut feelings. The connection is there between mother and child.

2. As the mother continued to receive the information, the connection grew stronger. Psychic abilities are developed in this way. It is an awareness of intuitive information and a willingness to work with it in a more profound manner. They are third dimension vibrations rooted in the earth plane and are easily accessed by psychic means. It can be strengthened over time, if applied. If the mother was psychic she received the information that way.

3. If the mother is a medium, she received the information in several ways: Connecting with her spirit guide, who sent her the information, or connecting directly to the spirit of the child. The method of connecting with vibrations goes in a different direction from psychic techniques. It is moving into the spirit realm, which has no boundaries like the third dimension does.

There is some controversy about receiving medium information through a connection of a living person. As I see it we have spirits whether our bodies are alive or dead. So a medium can connect with that spirit in any event.

I have done just that type of thing in the past. It can be very useful when looking for lost children.

The child may be alive or already passed over. Whichever it is, the spirit emanates in the same manner. The information is still there.

Now we can get into more detail about each subject to see their differences and similarities. It will be helpful for you to know these things when looking for a reader.

## *What Is Intuition?*

As I grew up, I always looked at nature for solid answers or confirmation to ideas. To understand something, it's easier to look at nature. God gave animals instinct to see them through their lives. He gave humans intuition.

I believe a human's intuition is comparable to an animal's instinct. The only difference is animals don't have society, human parents or teachers to discourage their instinctive abilities. Their natural feelings are not criticized. They are allowed to act on their gut reactions.

On the other hand, humans find it more difficult to deal with intuition. We are given intuition naturally, but constantly suppressed from using it.

For example, when a school teacher conducts a class, she must have a teaching plan already laid out, instead of allowing the flow of ideas to come intuitively, as the student's needs arise.

The term intuition is taken from the Latin root word, *intuerih*, which means to look within. But society always needs to have cold, hard facts to deal with things---not hunches.

When a lawyer works on a case, he must have evidence, not just a gut feeling. However, the gut feeling may be the one thing that helps him decide to take the case.

So after awhile, humans have turned away from intuition, tiring from having to always defend feelings, dreams and inner knowing.

To show the magnitude of intuition, I'd like to present some inspired information concerning animal instinct and human intuition.

Through this viewpoint, our connectedness with the animal realm and instinct is validated. Let's look at the events that could have happened to create the split between animals and humans, and how this influenced their evolution and ability to communicate through intuition.

Everything was created or manifested through energy by Creator Source. All substance and physicality shared the same atoms. So, we all (animals, humans and plant life) were of the same essence.

From the beginning of time, since all creation, life evolved in different ways as a result of experienced situations. But for a very long time, all remained as one, co-habiting perfectly.

Millions of years ago all breathing, sentient beings were in the infancy of humanity. This included animals and humans. For all practical purposes, there was no difference between the two. They were aware of outside occurrences, but did not "realize" that awareness.

We could call this inchoate consciousness: The basic movement towards humanity in its beginning stages.

It was at a very rudimentary starting point. For many generations, humans and animals lived on instinct and shared their spot together on earth.

Cohabitation was normal and created a base of paradigm thinking. This idea is based largely around oral folklore, which offers credence to traditional customs and beliefs.

An Okanogan Legend, "Creation of the Animal People," from the book *American Indian Myths and Legends*, selected and edited by Richard Erdoes and Alfonso Ortiz, shows the original spiritual connection of the two kingdoms.

As reported by Ella Clark in the 1950's, the legend tells of the earth being alive.

The Creator, known as Old One, made the ancient peoples. Some looked human and some were four legged. They all had great powers and the gift of speech.

The myths of that magical time when animals and humans shared cohabitation, tell there were no boundaries. Animals and Humans lived peacefully together and shared a common language. Being able to speak and hear through the eyes and ears of humans and animals combined, brought about a phenomenal essence of majesty and the divine.

Humans and Animals originally were one and the same. At a time when there was no judgment or comparison---that is, a time of love and acceptance---all living creatures were breathing the breath of the Creator. All was One. Humans, animals and plants all lived within the earth as one organism.

This combination of instinct/intuition allowed for the natural response to events and situations. Those actions (opposed to re-actions) were honored and respected.

35,000 years ago, our instinct was sharp and necessary. We relied on primordial knowing (an early form of instinct). Acting in a perfectly assimilated environment came easily. Re-action only occurred when the first knowing, or instinct, was doubted or thought out twice.

Re-action became a contrived response, not the natural one. After time, the human began to acknowledge self as separate. As humans evolved away from animals, they lost their primordial knowing. It diminished eventually to a state of mystery only a special few could tap into.

We, as humans choose not to rely on instinct in this day and time. Intuition is a luxury only some people feel the need to develop or even admit to. It somehow has taken on a frivolous and rather illusive connotation.

Our society has required more concrete means of maneuvering in this dimension. And many long forgotten abilities have become passé. The more we limit, the more we are boxed into paradigm issues.

Man is now on the move to seek out the well hidden gifts of instinct and intuition; however it will now represent itself.

Edgar Cayce is a modern day seer of prophetic events. Carl Jung, well known psychiatrist believed we can receive insightful information by tapping into the collective unconscious. Mona Lisa Schulz, M.D., Ph.D. is author of *Awakening Intuition,* is a neuropsychologist and neuroscientist. She has worked in the medical intuitive field for at least 12 years.

Her book is grounded in learning how to intuitively know about your own health and healing, and working with medical situations.

However Schulz spends much time describing how we are all intuitive to start with, and how to build on that intuitive awareness.

*~~ Want to Find Out More? Go to www.PsychicIntegrity.com and click on "Instinct vs. Intuition: Are They the Same?" ~~*

## What Is a Medical Intuitive?

The area of Medical Intuition is a delicate one. Never are we more susceptible to really damaging someone's life by giving the wrong information. Tiptoe in this area very carefully! While learning the spiritual mediumship techniques in the 1980s, I was told never to diagnose or prescribe. I feel that was very good advice.

Generally, a medical intuitive is able to find the cause of a physical or emotional condition. But to make a medical diagnosis is not usually an accepted methodology for medical intuitives.

To be true to the idea, we must go back in history. Thousands of years ago, the Greeks received their advice from oracles, which were systems of highly respected divination.

Indigenous groups of the world each have their own way of assisting the physically sick people of their clans. This may be through shamans or medicine men or women.

Recently, Edgar Cayce (as mentioned earlier) became very well know, as the sleeping profit. He lived in the first half of the Twentieth Century and was able to demonstrate channelled answers to questions on subjects such as health (as well as other things) while in a self-induced trance.Cayce entered into a trance-like sleep state. Then he answered the health question asked by the client.

The term and method known today as Medical Intuition was started in 1987. Dr. Norman Shealy and Carolyn Myss worked together in his practice. Dr. Shealy and Myss wrote the doctoral program at Holos University Graduate Seminary. Carolyn Myss is considered the first medical intuitive, officially using this term to describe what she does.

In 1988, Shealy and Myss co-authored a book titled, *Creation of Health*. After the book came out, Shealy recognized even though many people were calling themselves medical intuitives, they had no skill. He realized they needed to set verifiable standards to make the term credible and useful.

The American Board of Scientific Medical Intuition (ABSMI) started in 2000, by Dr. Shealy and Carolyn Myss. It is a nationally registered independent board.

The Board tests and certifies those who are proficient in the fields of Medical Intuition. The standards represent specific criteria for this aspect of Complementary, Alternative and Integrative Healthcare.

As defined by the Board, Medical Intuition is the science of intuitively assisting clients. This is done in cooperation with the primary health care professionals.

By using Intuitive Analysis and understanding their physical, emotional, mental and spiritual stress reactions, the Medical Intuitive works in cooperation with the client's physician or psychologist.

If a person's energy system is in a declining level and cannot be measured by conventional means (X-ray, blood test, etc.), the abilities of a medical intuitive can be used.

The intuitive determines any energy trauma while working in harmony with an allopathic medical team.

Since the ABSMI is the only certifying board in this field, the standard has been set. Anyone who is practicing as a medical intuitive (without training and credentials) runs the risk of improperly presenting information for a client.

There are intuitives who are expert at reading a client's physical condition and giving the correct protocol for clearing the situation. However, the best case scenario is to have someone with credentials and intensive training.

Always remember information given in this way is for counsel. After gathering as much information as possible, it is your decision that is important. Your health and perhaps your life are at stake here.

## *What Does Psychic Mean?*

Psychics access magnetic energy that comes from the human energy field, also known as the **aura**. They connect through sensing or viewing energy patterns in the field, recognizing anything going on in the person's life. The life energies of the past are there as well as potential possibilities being implemented in the higher realms, through intention and goal setting.

All people have a degree of psychic ability, as just explained with intuition. Some are aware of it and some are not.

Do you ever go to answer the telephone and already know who is calling (provided you don't look at your caller ID)? Do your dreams come true, even occasionally?

Have you ever felt like someone is looking at you at the grocery store, and when you turn around, a person down the aisle is staring at you?

These are examples of psychic abilities. It is simply knowing or sensing something without having other knowledge of it, or being able to logically explain how you know.

*SIDE COMMENT~*
*The psychic center, or the sixth energy center (also known as chakra), is called the third eye. It is located in the forehead, between the eyebrows. Psychic abilities come from using this energy center. The sixth chakra assists with clairvoyance, precognition, telepathy, and creative abilities.*

Many psychics are spiritually evolved individuals. But it is not a requirement to be psychic. Everyone has psychic ability. There are many levels of understanding and spiritual development. This information will help you determine if a certain reader is right for you.

The psychic reader who is in a high loving state, following his own spiritual direction will be a much better match for you, than someone who does it because he can. As in any profession, there are different levels of competency. This profession is no different.

Many successful, professional people credit their success to being psychic. They have a hunch about a certain merger or business plan. It's becoming more common for detectives to use psychic abilities when working on a case.

It is becoming much more acceptable to embrace your psychic abilities and use them as life tools, especially since television programs are introducing psychic and paranormal events.

Two areas psychic ability can be used are psychometry and precognition.

**Psychometry** is **picking up** or **reading** the energy of an object (such as keys, or jewelry) by holding it in your hand. You can sense the vibrations emanating from it. You receive information about the history of the object. If someone had it in his or her possession for a long period of time, you can receive information about that person as well.

The energy patterns of the object are downloaded into the reader's subtle bodies. The memories contained in the object are accessed by the subconscious mind and raised to conscious awareness.

Psychometry is used to heighten the contact of someone's vibration during a reading. Many readers use this method as a tool along with their main area of expertise. It also can be used to connect with others at a distance.

I have successfully used this method to assist contacting the spirit of a recently departed teenager, receiving critical information in locating the body.

**ESP or Precognition** is receiving information or knowledge of an event before it occurs. This is done by ESP (extra-sensory perception), through the dream state or by having a vision. Everything has a certain energy field to it. Thought forms also have a vibration that can be perceived.

The present moment exists because of past intention: The energy of intentions, thoughts and making plans move upwards in the energy body of the individual. These thoughts become manifest through the intention.

The same thing happens with the future. Let's say you are planning a trip to Europe in the fall of the year. Things are set into place. You hold the idea in your mind. The reader can sense this in your energy field. Possible events that might change the plans may also been seen.

The psychic reader works with the energy vibrations of the person involved. This is connecting with slower, earthly frequency vibrations.

In comparison, a medium works with spirit energy, or a lighter frequency than the earth plane, and connects with spirit entities, usually loved ones that have died. Psychics are not mediums, but mediums can also be psychic.

Psychics are in touch with the earthly vibrations of living people, especially those of close friends or relatives. This also includes being aware of spirit entities trapped or staying in the **astral dimension**.

The astral is inhabited by those not recognizing they have died, or wish to be close to the physical world. These entities or spirits do not see or want to be in the higher levels. They are usually spirits of people who have crossed over but hover close to what they know, love or care about.

There are also lower-vibration entities in the astral realm that are tricky to deal with. It's possible for a psychic can be cajoled into thinking they are connecting with higher frequency entities.

The astral realm has a lower subset of spirit energies. You should be aware of these energies to avoid them whenever possible. They can cause confusion. Discernment is very important in this area.

In our modern culture the word **psychic** comes from the Greek psychikos, meaning "of the soul, mental". It refers to the ability to perceive things hidden from the senses.

The term psychic also refers to theatrical performers using techniques such as prestidigitation, as in "psyching you out" and cold reading to produce the appearance of having such abilities. (More information about cold readings in the chapter "The Bottom Line" of this book.)

In the eighth century B.C., The Pythia or priestess presiding over the Oracle at Delphi, was well-known for information believed to be prophecies directly from Apollo. The position of Pythia was held by a succession of women selected from a guild of priestesses of the temple.

Some believe the frenzied delivery of information came from vapors rising from the ground. She spoke gibberish, believed to be the voice of Apollo. The gibberish was decyphered by priests into the prophecies preserved in Greek literature.

Other scholars believe the Pythia spoke intelligibly in her own voice. However, more recent geological investigations suggest ethylene gas was the means of Pythia's state of inspiration. No one can know with any certainty now.

Noted psychic Michel de Nostradame, the French apothecary had the ability to predict the future. Nostradamus was a seer who published collections of prophecies which were masked in symbolism in the 1500s. With his psychic powers, he predicted numerous major world events. His quatrains are studied to this day.

*~~ Want to Find Out More? Go to www.PsychicIntegrity.com and click on "Mechanics of Psychics" ~~*

## What Is Mediumship?

Mediumship is being aware of the vibrations of spirit beings, and receiving messages from them. It is the communication of a deceased loved one through an intermediary. The information is then given to those who are grieving the loss.

The main purpose is to provide recognition of continuing life after the physical death, and to send love and encouragement. Connecting with the crown chakra (or seventh energy system) at the top of the head, a bridge is built to the higher levels or planes of existence.

By building this bridge, an association is made with visions, imagination, and spiritual awakening. It enables you to empower your spiritual path. This opens you to integrity in becoming responsible·in your communication dealings.

Association with the higher realms also plants a firm foundation for the connection with finer vibratory entities and spirit teachers. Lower level energies will not be attracted to you, since you have established your connection with higher vibrations.

Other reasons spirit beings open communication with the living are to give evidential information only acknowledged by those still in the body. They create outward activities perceived by humans in a physical manner.

These activities are often recognized as paranormal activity. They manifest in physical form to be identified.

Mediumship involves cooperation between a living person and a person in the spirit realm. This entails either communication of some kind or physical manipulation of energies.

Mediumship is divided into two categories: mental (communication) or physical (energy manipulation).

**Mental mediumship** is communication by thought transference from the spirit to the medium. Mental information is communicated and then spoken by the medium. Information is brought to the medium as feelings, words, thought forms or impressions.

Depending on how deep the medium is under **control**, relates to how clearly the information is relayed: The deeper the control, the purer the information. Since spirit information flows through a living mind, with personal emotions, it could become clouded with personal influence by the medium.

*SIDE COMMENT~*
*Mediumistic Control has to do with the connection made by the spirit with the medium. There is a combination of energy used mentally and physically. The bond or link is made by the two through the consciousness of the medium. It can be a strong link or very light. The control is determined by the strength of the link. If the link is a good one, seasoned over time, different levels of trance can be manifested.*

Mediumship or communication with deceased loved ones can be very healing to those of us who are left here on earth. The person going through a grieving process needs evidence to prove there is life after death; that the loved one really is all right. There is a re-uniting of what appeared to be separated. Then closure begins.

The spirit has a real need to connect with their living loved one just to let them know he is alright. There is a reaching out by both parties to recognize the bond has not been broken, just changed.

Then the deceased loved one has an opportunity to share the experience of transition. It also gives comfort in the thought of death not ending life, but creates a new expansion of what life really is.

**Physical mediumship** is done with the use of physical energy. It is done under control as in the mental mediumship, but usually much deeper. The spirit manages the transformation of energy into physical objects, movement or sounds. A paranormal event occurs in the physical, and can be felt, heard or seen by humans.

This form of mediumship has to be the most unusual demonstration of what a spirit entity can do through medium control.

There have been far too many contrived and deceitful examples of the séance event. Because of that, many people discredit the entire concept of mediumship.

The spirit entity operating for the evidential séance uses both mental and physical energies of the medium to create a physical manifestation. This is something all sitters in the experience can witness physically.

The physical medium is one who has an over-abundance of a magnetic and etheric energy emanating as part of the aura/energy field of the individual. Usually, while the medium is in a deep trance state, the spirit being uses this etheric energy and creates **ectoplasm.**

If you have ever seen the movie "Ghost Busters" or any ghost-laden, scary program, you have seen a filmy or cloudy emanation coming from or around an entity, spirit being or ghost. This is the best representation of ectoplasm available.

*The Trance State: A deep control by the spirit will produce a trance state with the medium. A lighter trance is used for mental mediumship, while a deeper trance is used for physical mediumship.*

*Indicators for the trance state are similar to deep meditation. Trance can be recognized by the slow down of many of the medium's physical body activities which are generally controlled by the subconscious mind: heart rate, breathing and body temperature. It is not the same as the sleep state, but could be confused by it. For all intents and purposes, the medium is unconscious.*

*Since spirit speaks directly through the consciousness of the medium in the trance condition, the voice will sound much different than usual. This is considered more accurate information and is often called direct voice.*

*Channeling is a very mild form of trance, in which the medium is usually still awake and aware of the information coming through. It deals with higher spiritual teachings coming from the finer realms. As I see it, if you are unaware of the information coming through, you are in deep trance. If you are openly given a trail of information as a lecture or class, then you are channeling.*

Although the medium's etheric energy is the main source for the event, usually more is gathered from the sitters. If the energies are good, a large amount of ectoplasm is formed to work with. It takes full attention of everyone in the séance.

The use of personal, auric energy (full of emotional and feeling experience of the each person) is a main ingredient for this operation to be successful.

This is why the sitters in the séance not only experience the event, but actually become part of the event. It can be a very dramatic demonstration of spirit manipulation.

The medium gives consent to be used by the spirit being, by going into the trance state. The spirit is now in control of the work being done and can manipulate the ectoplasm to create phenomena.

A medium can produce physical phenomena because she has an abundance of this etheric ectoplasm. It is a part of the subtle energy body that allows us to emanate as humans.

In a physical medium, this subtle body is more loosely attached than in most people. (More on this in the chapter How You Can Talk to Heaven and How You Can't)

There is no limit to what can be done through physical mediumship, as long as the proper conditions are held in the séance room. These physical phenomena can range from rapping, levitation of objects or people, lights, independent writing/painting, **direct voice** (spirit speaks without the medium), and partial or full materialization of the spirit people.

I have witnessed and became part of many séances during my years in the work. I have seen a light show that would rival any rock star's concert!

I have seen **apports** (objects materialize out of thin air) in full view during the daylight. It truly is amazing what can be done during spirit control.

Why is it important to have physical phenomena? If the spirit mind (and we all have a spirit mind) can transform matter, then the same intelligence can transform other areas of life to manifest the world we know we could have.

Information is being shared about the Law of Attraction and Manifesting. This is another form of evidence to prove manifestation.

## *Mediumship Myths*

Here are some things that have been mistaken about mediumship:

*Myth:* There is something unnatural about mediumship
*Fact:* Mediumship is a very normal and natural ability. In fact, most people have at some degree the ability to sense spirit energies. For instance, you may recognize when you grandmother is around you because you smell something that reminds you of her powder.

*Myth:* It is a special gift given only to those who have attained a level of spiritual achievement.
*Fact:* Mediumship does not have to be attained after spiritual growth; however, it is best if it is. You can handle this ability better when you have a foundation in spiritual understanding. But mediums come in all sizes and shapes, as well as higher and lower levels of integrity. So be aware of who you are working with.

*Myth:* It has to do with miracles and magic.
*Fact:* Mediumship follows the precepts of all known spiritual laws. There is nothing magical about it.

*Myth:* It is used to read your mind or to control others.
*Fact:* Mediumship has nothing to do with mind reading. It is solely connection with those in spirit to bring comforting evidence of their existence.

*Myth:* Mediumship is a parlor game or a source of entertainment.
*Fact:* Mediumship is a serious endeavor and should be approached with dignity and respect. It is never to be used as a game or for entertainment purposes.

*Myth:* It is dangerous.
*Fact:* Practiced with responsibility and respect, mediumship cannot harm anyone! It is only the irresponsible practice of mediumship that can cause problems for the medium.

*~~ Want to Find Out More? Go www.PsychicIntegrity.com and click on "Want to Find Out What it's Like to be a Medium?" ~~*

# Chapter 3

## *How You Can Talk to Heaven and How You Can't*

# How You Can Talk to Heaven and How You Can't

*Understanding the Levels of Spirit*

As you grow up from a small child into adulthood, you are always introduced to the term, *heaven*. Normally, it is when a close loved one dies and your parents try to explain to you about the passing of life. They really don't know what it is or how to describe it. It usually ends up being a lovely place we all go when our bodies die. And Grandma is now an angel.

But over the years, we begin to believe heaven or the spiritual world is the only higher level of vibration separate from the physical world: all spirits in the spirit world are highly evolved beings. Quite often, while discussing this work, generalities are made. Psychic readers talk about "the material world" or "the spirit world". This is very limiting. It completely leaves out the majority of layers that represent the vibrations of spirit.

The world of spirit is used to convey all frequencies including that of loved ones who have died. But we tend to only think of our grandparents in the spirit world. The world of spirit is very vast and includes lower as well as, higher entities. You may be aware of angels and spirit guides in the reachable spirit realm of existence.

There are also expanded levels (or other heavens) with archangels and other highly evolved entities unreachable to mere mortals, such as in the Un-Manifest, Expressive, Causal, Mental, and Emotional Planes.

These planes do not need what we know as the laws of physics. Space and time do not exist outside of the physical world. Those of us in the body are the only ones who maneuver in the third dimension, and have no concept of what it would be like not to live here.

We are all part of one huge, dimensionless object made of things not of this world. Yet they are manifested in the elements of solid, liquid, gas and the ethers so we may live and understand them with physical recognition.

Our bodies are alive because they are temporarily inspirited within a time and space window. Our souls are eternally alive because they are eternally inspirited, part of the infinite existence of all.

As our awareness expands in life with the experiences we are having, we begin to see life as a whole: The wholeness of all of creation and interconnection with All. This symbolizes our idea of total consciousness.

## Chain of Command

To be able to understand how Spirit Communication works, it is first important to understand the different levels of spirit. This is something that is rarely spoken of or taught. A large number of readers, whether they are psychics or mediums, may not have any concept of where they are getting their information. To them, especially if there was no instruction, spirit is spirit and it must all be good. Nothing could be further from the truth.

To me, it could be risky not understanding the chain of command. As explained earlier, there are many trickster spirits in other realms and astral energies representing them selves as well known Biblical personalities, historical figures and even entertainers. These impersonators actually get their kicks by making you think they are who they say they are.

You, as a psychic reader, really want to believe you have connected with this popular entity, and ego takes over. One hosts the other and the charade continues. So let's get a better picture of how the layers of the World of Spirit can interact and how they cannot.

We all recognize ourselves as Spirit. That is important to realize as we discuss the process of progression into the third dimension. We actually descended into the third dimensional human incarnation. There are many identities formed from higher, more expanded energies and levels, as we made our way into the physical (material) world.

This is a quick list of the seven layers (or heavens) of existence starting from the highest to the lowest:

1. Un-Manifest or Celestial Plane
2. Expressive or Diamond Plane
3. Causal Plane (Atman)
4. Mental Plane (Buddhic)
5. Emotional Plane
6. Etheric Plane
7. Physical Plane (includes astral realm)

Going back into the beginning of time, or should I say, before the beginning, is the un-Manifest One or Creator Source (some may call God). As it recognized the desire to manifest, it did so as a field of being, consciousness and energy. There was no awareness of time, space or matter as we know it.

The only awareness was "I that I eternally Am". The ancient seers of India call this Brahman. As Brahman found outer awareness as an individualized expression, the form of the "I AM" (atman or monad) was achieved. This is the elementary individual spiritual being reflecting within itself the whole of the universe.

This is still what we consider before the beginning. Atman became distinct from Brahman but not separate from it.

The second plane of existence is where Archangels, the overseers of Creator Source reside. The archangel realm is known as Dhyani-Chohan, a collective host of seven spirit beings. They are recognized by religious orders in different ways: Angelic Hosts in Christianity, and the Messengers of the Jewish faith. They are also known in Theosophy as "the Gods" of Genesis who created Adam and Eve.

The Dhyani-Chohan is considered the Intelligent Force that gives to and relates Nature's laws and is the vehicle for manifestation of the divine or universal thought and will. They regulate and care for the higher Power (Un-Manifest Plane).

Expressive Plane is just that: a desire of expression. A kind of transport or means of conveyance was created so Atman could be self-actualized. Planes and dimensions were created as the vehicles to move and explore.

Spirit began to express itself in an external way. Eventually, a universe with time and space was created. This allowed for infinite possibilities of expression and creation of forms, to interact with each other (as opposed to within itself).

On our journey to third dimension, the pure I AM Presence created reflections of itself, interacting and moving more directly in the denser dimensions.

Some were human, some angelic (devic or elemental). As this movement progressed, one section of The Presence created an over-soul of human-ness, and moved further into human soul consciousness.

Since soul manifested after the creation of time and space, it oriented itself into specific form, and maneuvered in space-time constructs.

Expressing self was the main directive, so Spirit created personalities. The personalities had mind and emotion, drawn from the Mental and Emotional Planes, which had already been created.

It continued to move into denser form and subtle bodies, interacting with other personalities. That is when we incarnated as souls within personalities to explore the world of form.

This is still in the fifth or Emotional Plane, and we were still unified with aspects of soul, over soul and monad. The soul still had creator consciousness. It moved into the sixth or Etheric Plane and merged with the angelic (devic and elemental) kingdoms, creating infinite life forms in physical realms.

The Elohem are part of the angelic realm. They created planets and special levels of creation orders: nature spirits (such as Pan) and human bodies. Soul was still unified with all other aspects of self from the descent from Original Source.

We, as spirit, had twelve DNA strands at this time. They represent two strands from each plane that we traveled through (Un-Manifest, Expressive, Causal, Mental, Emotional and Etheric) on our way to the physical world. With these twelve strands, we were able to attune ourselves to and maneuver within all of those planes.

As we continued to move into more specific expression, we came to the seventh or Physical Plane. This is where the Third Dimension exists. At the time of decent we fragmented from the Source and experienced ourselves as separate. Access to higher frequencies, over-soul and atman were literally cut off. The angelic awareness separated from human personality, and a split was created within our bodies.

Angelic (Elemental) awareness maintained control of all the autonomic functions (heartbeat, breathing, hormonal balance, etc.) Personality maintained the voluntary functions.

## The Fall

Our DNA fragmented too. Two strands from the Etheric Plane fell into the Physical Plane frequency and the other ten were cut off from us. We were not able to access those planes as physical humans. We still are part of them, but unable to access them.

We fell away from all five of these consciousness levels. In order to move into these dimensions again, we must be able to embrace them. This means a time when we can re-integrate with the five elements and reclaim the lost ten strands.

Because we only have two active DNA strands, our brain at this time only seems to be able to access the "beta" or waking personality of our human-ness. We are still a part of the One, but not able to connect with it.

The beings that inhabited and created the other five dimensions are still part of who we are. But we have moved our consciousness from Un-Manifest One into this third dimension.

We are one with that un-manifest beginning and all the other manifestations that grew from there. We are one with all, but detached from it through the physical existence.

You can understand why it would not be humanly possible to connect or commune with entities or energies residing in the much higher planes, since we were cut off from them; literally stripped of the gear (DNA strands) that made it possible.

In a very crude, but understandable analogy, I compare it to a baby still in the mother's womb, with out an umbilical cord. The baby is still part of the wholeness of the mother but without any means of communication: totally disconnected.

The only way to communicate with an Archangel from beyond the Causal Plane would be if we bumped up our energies and frequencies.

We would have to raise it to a very unsustainable level, and possibly connect with a fraction or lesser element of the Archangel. Not having the proper DNA to access those areas, we could not withstand a lengthy contact without totally exploding, or combusting in some way. Burn out would occur since the third dimension physical body is too heavy and dense to hold the finer frequency.

Many people sincerely believe they are communing with Archangels and other beings from the Expressive and Causal Planes. With the information shared in this book, you can easily see the entities they are connecting with could be masquerading as Archangels.

It is not possible to exist in the physical world and be controlled by an enlightened being. (Being under control is an essential part of spirit communication, including channeling) The two things cannot vibrate at the same level.

I believe it would be impossible to connect with an Archangel or other highly evolved entities. There may be a connection to trickled-down knowledge or funneled information relating to Archangels. However, the vibrational mechanics don't seem to allow for the direct connection with Archangels.

It is possible good information is shared. However, be very aware of what level you are accessing. Only accept what you know and feel are appropriate spirit energies. You must question…always question what you are receiving.

The only realm or plane we can commune with right now is the plane right next to our own: the Etheric Plane. The Etheric and Physical Planes are bridged with the Astral Realm. This is where our loved ones reside.

The blended areas of Astral and Etheric also house spirit guides, our past life personalities and guardian angels. Some believe, and I tend to agree, that Ascended Masters and the **Akasha Repository** are also within our reach there.

Within this Etheric Plane, besides the guides and loved ones that we communicate with, are also lower entities and energies. This can be a collection of negative thought forms, random tricksters, and the spirits of low-level individuals. They want to stay connected in a physical way and are focused on causing confusion on the physical plane. It is necessary to be aware of these levels so you can avoid them.

The more you question the entities you connect with the more information you will find out. Always ask direct questions and require they give you truthful answers. Be sure you are connected with only the highest entities. The rest have nothing positive for you.

## Opening Up

It's interesting how a medium opens up to receive information from a spirit entity. This work is dealing with and being aware of subtle energies. The more you use it, the more your subtle energy fields (or etheric and emotional bodies of the aura) open up to connect with the entity. This is not the normal condition for the aura of most people. Those who do not engage in this type of work have very tightly connected subtle bodies, as they were designed to be.

During the unfoldment process, mediums adjust their energy fields to accommodate the phenomenon of spirit communication. This can be done in a very safe manner if taught over a long period of time.

I know, it sounds very strange. Mediums from the earlier days (1800-1950) allowed their whole essence to be used by the spirits of loved ones who passed over. They were willing to let the outside entity take full control of the body and aura. This proved to be very harmful to the medium over a period of time.

Several things happened as a result of prolonged control: on a small scale, the medium in question trusted the entity so much she allowed the control to take place on a regular basis.

She lost all control of her own faculties, or five senses. When you rely too much on an outside source, you lose your own ability to reason things out.

Another result of allowing constant spirit control is the physical body and emotional aspect of self is deteriorated. I saw it happen in my early years of study. Several mediums enjoyed the attention and financial gain of producing séances.

They engaged the spirit entity much more than should be: Usually giving two séances each day for two or three days in a row.

The physical body cannot deal properly with this practice because it is not a physical event. So it takes a period of time to recuperate from it. Many mediums have developed early diabetes as a result of repeated use as an instrument or died at an early age.

The emotional aspect is in peril. The emotional body in the aura helps the development of the person—the ability to deal with issues of the world in a normal manner. If the emotional body is constantly adjusted to accommodate spirit communication, it becomes shifted out of place, or loose, resulting in the inability to deal with things in the physical world.

There is speculation as to why some people become mentally unstable. Many mental patients think they are well known personalities or hear voices telling them to do upsetting things. Their subtle bodies may have become detached, therefore, making it difficult to deal with the physical world, and open to the control of outside entities.

Spirit communication is a viable tool dealing with grief. It can be used in verifying the case of life after death. Many people need to know their relative is alright and in a good place. We need to realize the information coming from the spirit of a loved one is not necessarily highly evolved.

So, why am I a medium? How do I deal with the conditions I just described? I do not invite spirit entities to inhabit my body or being. When I am in a session with a client, I work through my spirit doctor (highly evolved guiding force that is still in the higher astral realm). I have become familiar him and consider him an aspect of myself.

I work with the spirit energy of the client and receive information for her/him. If I am asked to connect with someone in particular, I go through my spirit doctor. That extension of me connects with the loved one in question and filters information down to me. Once in awhile I connect directly with a spirit entity for a specific purpose.

When I do connect without the benefit of the filter, believe me, it is very intense. Any emotional trauma or physical problem can be felt or experienced by the medium during this time. It's as if you are experiencing it yourself and very difficult to move away from.

It is definitely not something I would enjoy doing on a regular basis. It is difficult to disconnect from the emotional trauma. I can see why it would pull energy from the medium and leave her in a state of confusion. There would have to be a period of adjustment.

The information I've shared here is very sketchy concerning the different levels of spirit or planes of existence, to say the least. I have taught it in my Spiritual Awakening Class for five weeks in a row, and barely scratched the surface.

There are many books and resources that delve into the levels of The Spirit World. Many are of different religions and cultural understandings with different words and meanings, as well as different interpretation. So it can be confusing to sift through.

Check the Resource Section in the back of this book for a more detailed study of this subject, if you are interested. I've tried to condense it in a manner to make the point of communication with the Spirit World and what that really entails.

It all boils down to the awareness of what information you are receiving and how it feels. Discernment is everything.

# Chapter 4

## *Creating Your Foundation*

# Creating Your Foundation

Metaphysical or spiritual gifts can be developed by regular exercises to strengthen them. Take notice of what you are seeing, hearing and feeling --- and really pay attention to it. Ask your Guides (Higher Self) what it means, or if there is more information. Then listen.

This chapter is essential in preparing yourself with integrity and being able to hold the energies and vibrations of spirit properly. Each section here only touches on areas to work with. Please follow up with more intensive study on your own.

Knowing self is the first rule. Be physically aware of your body-temple and providing the proper environment for your spirit to live in. Explore your emotional self through uplifting lessons on positive thinking and expression. And it can be through the mind, by studying transformation, **psycho-navigation**, self hypnosis and journaling.

## A Proper Approach

First we must look at the basic premise of unfoldment. It is the continued growth or allowance of the spirit to manifest in your life. Spiritual Discovery is paramount in any unfoldment process and is the first intention for becoming psychic.

The more your inner spiritual core of being is set as a foundation all other things can prosper and grow. Your power as a spirit being human is very great and it must be your first endeavor to seek this self-knowledge and understanding.

It has been said that spiritual values are: patience, love, compassion, maturity, respect, appreciation, intelligence, harmony, inner peace, joy and a dedication to what is often called the good, the true and the beautiful.

I believe that to be true. However, I believe all the above values are components of one aspect humans must embrace: Love. To know Love is to understand the spiritual unity of all Life. Once you recognize you are one with your neighbor and enemy, it is impossible to perform a hateful act against him. It would be just like doing it against you.

All life and matter are manifestation of the one immortal self, the universal mind. This mind cannot chastise itself, fight with or destroy itself. We are all created from one intelligence. We all return to one intelligence.

Seemingly, we are separated from it by being in the physical body, and desire to know this complete unity again. It is to this emotional drive we give the name: LOVE. This is the spiritual development to address before any serious psychic development is sought. You must be solid in your understanding of who you truly are and how to tap into your Divine Source.

At this point, I believe it is important to say I am not speaking of religion, per se. Rather; I am talking about your relationship with your True (Higher/Inner) Self. This is the connection with the creative universal source. Just to acknowledge it is not enough, but to develop the relationship and feel comfortable working with it all the time.

The main areas to start with are: meditation, self-exploration, emotional release and non-judgment concepts. These all surround the idea of Love (loving self).

This is my idea of Integrity and Moral Ethics. All other ethical areas can be covered after this main premise is embraced.

Preparing yourself in a spiritual manner is the first step for progressing in any psychic or intuitive endeavor. Do not just run head long into anything---especially something this serious.

Whenever you are dealing with the energy of another person or any spirit entities, you better have your head on straight at the beginning. This is a spiritual activity. It's important to understand how you are connected to life, spiritually.

While looking at the possibility of becoming psychic or mediumistic, it might help to understand it has always been with you. The gift has been embedded into your being from before birth.

All living things have some sort of perceptive abilities. Of course the Animal Kingdom uses instinct. Humans also have a similar ability. Every one is intuitive. But it depends on how much you pay attention to it and use it, as to how well you develop it.

*There grows a most remarkable thing*
*In the most unusual place.*
*You may never imagine it*
*To be hiding in this space.*

*But Someone with much Wisdom*
*Knew just the thing to do---*
*Put it somewhere special*
*So it can never be lost from you.*

*~~~Soul of the Universe Guided Meditation*

*You have always been connected with the Source. Now it is time to get   familiar with communicating with it and recognizing it as such.*

## We Are All Searching

As spirit beings, we are incarnated into the physical body and our memory of being spirit fades. The physical experience we have takes all our attention away from those memories. As a result, we know there is something missing from our existence. We try reaching outside of ourselves for the answer, living the dream rather than the reality.

So, our search for self begins.

Much of the information shared here will be through many of my experiences, visions and teachings. Personal experience is the best way I can relate the information to you.  Even though I relate most of it as intuitive experiences and readings for others (permission granted from the clients), it is all about learning how the information comes to you, and how to present it.

*Letter received September 21, 1999:*
*Dear Melissa,*

*Thank you for being the vehicle by which my request was answered. I recently attended the Whole Life Expo in Minneapolis, of which you were a speaker. I went to the expo wanting some reassurance that my husband, who died May 8, 1998, five months after being diagnosed with pancreatic cancer, was okay.*

*I listened to you speak and was drawn to you, so I signed up for a reading. At the last hour, I chickened out and didn't go.*

*Unbeknownst to me, my sister, Lila, also signed up with you. The first thing you saw in her reading was a guitar being played by or belonging to someone in the spirit world. The only person Lila knew of was my husband Bruce.*

*You also saw a white flower. Lila didn't know that I have a white silk rose that was Bruce's in a vase next to his urn of ashes. I'd also put white flowers at his memorial marker and on his parents' gravesite.*

*I'm beginning to think that my task here on earth is to have faith in the unknown. My strong Lutheran upbringing didn't prepare me for all this. I'm slowly learning that there is a lot more out there than I was taught and to keep open to possibilities. Thank you once again.*

*With Love to All, Jeanette*

This is just one of many letters that have been such blessings to me. It confirms what I have always known: Our deceased loved ones are always around us. They are eager to communicate with us in whatever way they can.

Even though Jeanette was not raised understanding what existence is like after the physical death, she was willing to be open to it. Her hesitation at the last minute did not deter her husband from making him self known from the other side. He presented solid clues in her sister's reading that Jeanette would understand.

This reading was not presented in a sensational way, but in more of a learning experience Jeanette was more open to.

After giving spiritual intuitive readings and teaching spiritual concepts to many people over the past 30 years, I have come to understand one thing: We are all searching. We may not always know what it is we are looking for. But one thing is certain. We know there is something more. There is something more than the physical existence we recognize in our lives.

Going to work everyday, coming home to prepare supper, taking the kids to their lessons, and going to bed, just to start it all over again the next day--- is not all there is to our lives. There must be something more we can't really see on first inspection.

The trials and errors, and training I relay in this section on the preparing for the unfoldment process should used as a method of coming in touch with the part of yourself you may be seeking.

There will be times you will only be able to rely on one person--- yourself. It will be imperative it is the True Self you confer with. You will then know for sure what no one else has told you.

## Illuminating Moments

We all have moments of reverie. You know, those few seconds when everything seems to disappear from your thoughts. The only thing that has your attention is a feeling of a special, warm, inner knowing: almost a universal understanding of life. But it only lasts a few seconds. Then it is gone, shaken off by reality. Then we go along with life, status quo and forget the special illuminating moment.

Where did you go? What was going on during that moment? If you were in class at the time, your teachers would call it daydreaming, or entertaining distracting thoughts. Perhaps your parents would call it just your imagination. But while you experienced it, the moment was the only thing real, not a dream. And the world (or life, if you will) seems to be the distraction. We keep looking for this other part of our lives.

The famous illusionist, Harry Houdini (after having many issues with fakery and being disillusioned with mediums) and his wife organized an elaborate way of testing the existence of life on the other side. They made a pact with each other, using a special code of words. Whoever passed from life first would make every effort possible to communicate the code to the other. This was to be accomplished through a spirit medium.

After Houdini died, his wife traveled from one medium to another, looking for the correct words to be given. There is quite a story involved in her search. But in the end, supposedly, she told the code to someone in confidence.

As a result, she was scammed into thinking that a (deceitful) psychic brought the true Houdini into the circle. I believe that she died later, never really feeling like she had contacted her husband.

How sad that story is. If she had just quieted herself, she probably would have been able to commune with Houdini, on her own. Instead, she looked outside of herself for the contact.

Another example of how different people understand where the soul goes after death is from a wonderful movie called, "Nell". It stars Jody Foster as a young girl living in the remote mountains of Tennessee. She did not know other people, and her mother kept her hidden away for her safety.

She spent every waking moment of her young life with her sister, who later died by accident far off in the woods.

Nell left her sister's body where the accident happened. She kept fresh flowers on her sister's eyes. Nell could not bear to see her gone and did not understand why her sister did not live. She continued her sister's life as a daydream of them together, as before. Her sister's spirit was with Nell, in her heart's memories.

It's very interesting to see how we react to death and dying and we all deal with it in the best way we know. It is important to process through it all. The grief process is a rite of passage for those who still live. It gives us the proper amount of time and space to recognize what happened and how to fit our lives back together. A medium can be helpful in assisting the grieving person with evidence of the loved one's continued existence.

The quest for the missing part of lives can be seen in our Bible, Quran, Dead Sea Scrolls, Nag Hammadi Library, Bhagavad-Gita, many other sacred writings, and prose and poetry of the ages. They speak of the promise of another life: Of insurmountable love, of peace that passes understanding.

We see the search for truth in the diversity of religions of the world, showing the many ways man has searched.

We see it in the race to get into outer space. We see it with research scientists testing paranormal occurrences; our astronomers who are constantly looking and listening to our skies.

After all this looking outside of ourselves, I believe humankind will find what we are searching for. But the answer will not be out there.

The answer is in the one place which has kept the secret so well. The material world has done a wonderful job of keeping us blind to the real world.

## What is Your Focus?

What is the main focus in your life? Is it finding a job, or keeping the one you've got, just to pay the rent every month? Or is it searching for the special someone who can make you happy?

Society has evolved a way of believing that keeps us always limited to the physical plane. Stuart Wilde, noted author of *The Winds of Change*, among other revolutionary books, tells us of what he terms "the tribe". We all belong to a tribe: a group of peers we relate to in some way or other.

We may be Methodist, Italian, a wood-worker, a member of the Smith family, a woman, a mother, a homeowner, so on. Each group we belong to dictates, to a certain extent, what we will think, what we will wear, where we are to live, and how we make a living. It will try to keep us in a tidy little box.

Whenever we have a new idea, the tribe will not allow us to follow through with it. It keeps us close to what is known and understood. The tribe is threatened by anything unknown.

It keeps everything stable and secure. A thought outside of the box could ruin the whole paradigm of the tribe. The very existence of the tribe would be threatened if things changed too much or too fast.

Being part of the human tribe, keeps us all working very hard just to make a living.

Television and printed media produce marketing techniques through commercials and regular programming and news reports that keep our minds directed at purchasing. All we strive for all day long is to purchase what the tribe determines as necessary.

We become so driven to succeed in material wealth and external relationships we find no time for spiritual growth. Despite that distraction, there still is a hunger to satisfy, to look for the purpose in life. It seems all this rush to succeed should lead us to something. But lead to what?

So we search. There is a basic Christian and Judaic belief "the soul is eternal and returns from whence it came." But somehow, even though this is a creed of these religions, the church does not bring this truth to light in an effective way.

In answer I say, you should never take for granted what has been told to you. But take it upon yourself to read, study, question, go within, and then come to your own conclusion.

Sacred texts were brought into existence for a reason. If you study two or more, you begin to see similarities, not differences. They speak of heaven, nirvana, and some kind of life after death.

We all have an essence that flows to its source when released. That source itself is life giving. Since the use of the words *life* and *death* are terribly limiting in themselves, we wrestle for a better understanding.

## *Giving Up the Physical*

Grandma lived with our family for six or seven years after Grandpa died. Over time, she had small strokes. When they first started, it was almost comical, the odd things she reasoned out.

She brushed her teeth with Brill Cream hair gel instead of toothpaste. They both came in tubes, so it seemed fine in her mind to use either one. Her mind was not always working properly. But she still knew all the words to her favorite song, "In the Garden".

Grandma was a fiercely protective individual. It was her mission in life to make sure everyone and everything in her control area was all right. She was constantly checking on my younger sisters and me, making sure we were in the right place. If outside in December, making snow angels, she was afraid we passed out from cold exhaustion. And insisted we come in to warm up.

Preparing the daily dinner was her territory. She was in control of Mom's kitchen. Mom made excuses to go to the grocery every afternoon, to give Grandma some space.

Time went by and her prized violets began to wilt from lack of attention. She sat in the rocker for hours. Soon she lost control of her bodily functions. Then randomly she wandered off down the road without our knowledge.

It got to the point Mom couldn't do everything needed for Grandma anymore. The difficult decision was made to move her to a nearby nursing home.

When Grandma finally lost all control, and her controlling area was gone, she let go, and released her wonderful essence so it could flow back to its source.

We knew she was ready. We were ready too. It was almost a welcome relief. So it wasn't difficult to let her go.

About five years later, my dad told my husband and me something interesting. He said about a week after Grandma passed away, he saw her.

She was standing in the archway between the hall and dining room. She stood arms folded, and surveyed the area (her control area). She stood there for several minutes, just looking around, making sure everything was all right. Then she faded away.

It was good to know she was in control again. Her mind and memories were restored to her in that wonderful divine source. She was really okay. Grandma's spirit was tired of trying to make her physical body maneuver in the mundane world, so it let loose of the body and flowed back to its source.

## You Are Already Spirit

After the death of the body, you don't "go into spirit". This way of saying it is just easier to explain. The literal truth is you always have been spirit. You come into this world to experience the physical body. You are already spirit.

You take on this physical suit, mainly because it works best in the third dimension. You are still spirit, but living in a body. When the physical body dies away, it gives up the ghost, and the spirit continues.

A great way for you to gain experience as spirit is to see it through the physical form. You get better understanding about life and what it has for you, by personal experience.

In this way you learn how to perceive memories as messages. This is one way spirit speaks to you.

The whole idea of understanding about life and learning about messages leads us to the term "medium": that which lies in the middle.

*Medium* means through which anything is accomplished; a person sensitive to ultra normal elements with the ability to convey information of some sort. To me, that is a go-between.

I have been a go-between for many years, for many people, including myself. I see now, how important it is to be able to access Spirit information and wisdom to assist me on my path.

The story I share with you now may seem a little strange, but it really encapsulates many situations you may have had during your childhood years, but perhaps ignored because it was so unusual.

My path to recognizing spirit has been a long one. I remember as a child of three and four, talking in my mind to other entities. My bedroom door was made of wood. I believed the figure of swirls in the grain of the wood was a friend.

The door spirit listened to everything I said. It had compassion for my plight as a youngster, and gave me solace. There was a special feeling for that being. To this day, I recognize it as being spirit of some kind.

This illustrates how communication can be. It seems as if you make up the dialog, but believe me, it is real.

I spent many hours a day outside as a youngster, before my sisters were born. Those seven years represented the time I still remembered what it was like to be spirit.

I shared many conversations with spirit in my mind as I walked and ran out in the country setting of our home. With no children near us, and not much connection with my parents, it was left up to me to be my own companion.

There was an old, tapped out gravel pit adjacent to our property. The rocks and ground there shared many secrets to me. At that time, I did little talking.

Many hours were spent in mental communion with the energies of the earth. It's rather difficult to explain. Only ideas or concepts were interchanged. I had a "knowing".

I believe this is what helped me stay clairsentient. It probably is why I am still so passionate about Mother Earth.

The early years of your life create a foundation for the rest of your existence. It frames who you are and where you will go. As you go back in your memory, spend some time visiting your early childhood. What lessons did you learn? How does this relate to your present experiences? Delve into your Inner Self and know yourself as whom and what you truly are.

This inner knowing helps you form a spiritual reverence to your study of psychic abilities. Whatever you are experiencing or learning in the present, be sure to take it within yourself and study it there too.

# Chapter 5

# *The Working of Vibration*

# The Working of Vibration

Divine Source created All of Life, the whole of the universe. It was manifested through perfection. So all atoms are created or manifested as perfection. No matter what is made with them, they must, by logic, be perfect. If we look to science for an explanation of matter, we see everything has vibrational frequency according to its nature. It is made up of molecules and atoms.

These atoms vibrate at different rates, and therefore produce different things: the human body, a tree, jello, a computer, the kitchen sink, or living room wall. All these are made out of atoms. They all vibrate at different rates, making it jello or a sink. It depends on the rate of vibration as to how dense or solid the object is.

No matter what it is, the vibration is perfect for what it is. The same holds true with the way we look at a situation, person or thing. If you believe a situation to be good, that is how you will experience it. If the person you meet, you see as negative, that is how you will relate to him.

## *Look at the Perfection*

I always encourage clients, workshop attendees and development students to view the person or situation as originating in perfection, instead of the negativity.

After seeing the perfection and accepting it that way, imagine what could have happened to the person to make him seem so negative? What circumstances could he have experienced, and what things must have been said to him as a young child, to create such a mass of misery?

If we get past the misery covering their God light, you can remember how perfect the person really is. That is the part that can be loved. That's God.

That is the only part we are required to love. The part in misery does not have to be addressed. By not paying attention to it, it actually does not exist.

We are also covered by the result of thinking. The way we re-act to circumstances through out life, will cloud the aura. It confuses the way we look at life and the way life sees us.

## *The Aura and Chakra System*

When studying energy and vibrations, it is important to understand the aura and chakra system. It is necessary to know how vibrations influence the energy field around a person when you are unfolding your spiritual gifts.

The human is a three-fold being: body, mind, spirit. Within the being are many subtler areas.

There are areas of the human that do not appear as obvious as the physical or mental aspects. But we still deal with them on a regular basis.

The physical body is animated through the chakra system. In major realms of thought, and for introductory purposes, there are seven charkas for the human body. Other cultures have different ideas on this, but generally it is accepted there are seven.

The seven charkas correspond to physical parts of the body. But it also deals with how we express ourselves: how we feel, think and act. It manages the physical wellness and connects us with our divine selves.

The word charka means "wheel of light" in Sanskrit. Each wheel is an energy vortex and helps animate life to function as a physical being. The spirit must have a physical vehicle to maneuver in the third dimension.

These subtle areas are other bodies that help us gain awareness of things around us. They are controlled by the seven charka centers. Each center is represented by a color. These colors make up the aura, or auric field.

*"She's green with envy." "I'm so angry I can see red." "It's blue Monday." "...purple mountains majesty."*

All these colors denote feelings. Where did the phrases and color companions come from? They came from the aura. The aura is an electro-magnetic field surrounding the physical body. It is also around plants, animals and inanimate objects. The aura is a manifested part of the body, an extension of the spirit.

The way life is perceived and the way we experience feelings through the power centers is expressed in the field around us with different colors. They are merely different vibrations.

If you were angry with someone, an intuitive person could feel or receive those angry vibrations around you. In the same manner, a person who can see or read the aura colors may see anger colors (perhaps red, since anger quite often comes from the baser instincts) around you.

Life giving energy emanates outward from the physical body and is seen as different colors.

## Emotions and Auras

The special energy field around the body contains everything we think and experience. Those who see or feel the aura can sense your feelings. You walk around like an open book. Your emotions, likes and dislikes, all your thoughts are right there around you for anyone and everyone to see or feel.

If you stop and think about it for a minute; you might change your thinking. Everyone has thoughts about people and situations. We consider those thoughts private, or even secret. If the truth be known, there is no private thought. It is all right there in your aura.

Going a step further, the old saying, "thoughts are things" is proven by the aura. Each thought you have comes into your vibration because it is attracted there. The aura around you is vibrating at a certain rate because of the thoughts you have.

The more you think a certain thought (say, "Today's Monday, I never feel good on Monday's") the closer you bring it into your being. Until sooner or later, it manifests in the physical, and you really don't feel good.

When I am consulting for a client, I am working with these vibrational fields. That is what I sense around them.

If the situation I vision is not already happening, I know it will be within the next two weeks. This is the amount of time I sense within their auric field. They are actually pulling the situation into their lives.

If we were spirit alone, the perfect manifestation of the Supreme Source, our auras would be a clear sparkling glow. But since we are spirits of the Divine Essence, experiencing human form in this earthly realm, we must constantly strive for perfection. As a result, our auras are multi-colored, as we learn our lessons from day to day.

## Changing the Energy Field

In her book, *Excuse Me, You're Life Is Waiting*, Lynn Grabhorn challenges us to actually change our energy fields. She says if you have a negative response in life, with nothing going your way, she has an antidote.

We get engrossed in the negative actions in life. After awhile, it becomes a vicious circle. Since what we think is attracted to us, we seem to manifest the negative circumstances into our lives. The negative thing is in our life and that is what we think about. You see the circle?

But Grabhorn says to focus on something positive. It could be how you felt at the amusement park when you were seven years old. I know from personal experience how difficult this can be! But if you can enjoy the thought for 16 seconds, it actually alters the electro-magnetic vibration around you. That means the aura has changed. What you have around you is now positive vibration. This positive vibration actually pulls other positive things in to your life.

## The Chakras

Now let's look at the energy centers called chakras.

*First Chakra* is known as the base or root chakra, centered at the base of the spine. It is represented by the color red. It controls the physical body, through the reproductive organs and influences concepts and new ideas. The first chakra keeps us aware of our surroundings and aware of how to survive in those surroundings.

*Second Chakra* is called the sacral chakra; it is the color orange. It rules the emotional body through the lymphatic system and deals with initial feelings or emotional issues. Everything experienced in the world is first acknowledged through the second chakra.

*Third Chakra* is known as the solar plexis. It is yellow and governs the mental body around the adrenals. It influences opinion. This area perceives the feelings coming through the sacral chakra, and judges it in some way. It uses intellect to discern the truth in all situations.

*Fourth Chakra* is known as the heart center. The green colored chakra controls the astral body through the thymus. It gives you a second feeling, usually through the love emotion. It deals with love and its other cousins: joy, happiness, etc. This chakra allows loving life and others without attachments.

*Fifth Chakra* is the throat in the color blue. It rules the etheric body. The thyroid is involved in expression of self, through the voice, art, and writing. Speaking your truth is not for anyone else's information, but a chance to honor your true self.

*Sixth Chakra* is the third eye recognized by the color indigo. It works with the celestial body through the Pineal Gland. It influences inspiration and insight.

It creates visions, both clairvoyantly and as future goals, tuning into intuition to find truth concerning life circumstances.

*Seventh Chakra* is the crown or top of the head. It is represented by violet purple. The Ketheric body is associated with the pituitary gland and works with release and surrender. It connects us to our Universal Divine Wisdom. Imagination can be used to prepare goals and create a stronger self image.

## The Heart Bridge

The heart charka is a gateway holding the third dimension, the physical self, together with the higher dimension, our spirit self.

Anger and upset can be experienced during the day's activities in a routine manner. Certain situations lend themselves to hostility, resentment and emotional upset. Holding onto anger, fear and hatred can be a very risky thing to do. There are ways of seeing this and correcting it before any damage is done. It's alright to feel experiences and learn from them: Then released.

Are they emotions or feelings? After investigating these terms, I realize society has misunderstood the meaning of the two words. To often we think of emotions and feelings as being the same. I believe they are different.

Feeling is a sensed action to a life experience. It is a totally honest response. It is something meant to be realized or acknowledged, through the physical experience. Perhaps it is an awakening to understand a situation more deeply.

*Feelings* should never be denied. They need to be experienced, looked at, worked through and released. Feelings are experienced through the lower half of the body and its charkas.

This area represents and controls the third dimensional aspect of the whole being. The second charka is actually called the seat of the emotional body, with its contents being feelings. It should probably be called more aptly the feeling body, as referenced to the physical portion of the body.

*Emotion* on the other hand is something different. In my understanding, the only true emotion in this life is love. The Universe created Spirit through pure love. The only driving force of life is love. There is no such thing as unconditional hate or unconditional envy. All the great spiritual teachers spoke of love. When a small child is asked about God, he will say, "God is live."

The heart has long been the symbol of love. But it is more than a feeling for your parents of spouse. It also includes joy, ecstasy, compassion, happiness, satisfaction and honor. These are all cousins of love.

The heart charka, being the next level beyond third dimensional existence, is the first charka of the astral body. It actually cushions or bridges the material and spiritual worlds. According to Rosalyn Bruyere, in her book, *Wheels of Light, A Study of Chakras*, the heart contains second feelings, which are quite different than the first (as demonstrated in the second □harka). The heart also contains transformation.

I believe the heart area of the astral body, which connects the physical and spiritual realms, gives us a second chance to look at the action to life experiences. Now we can look through the eyes of the Creator, with love for the Universe.

We are part of the whole of the universe. Since the universe is always growing, expanding and becoming All It Can Be, spirit beings in human form are set into place to share their life experience with the universe.

The Universal Creator cannot experience life on earth as a physical form in any other way. We are the extension of Mother-Father God.

*Keep it At Arms Length*
The human experience is connected to the Creator by a pure silver cord of love. This is the only way life experiences can be directed back to the Universe—through love. It's the only language Spirit understands. The love emotion is the only way to put all earth experiences and feeling into correct perspective. Whenever life action is experienced, the feelings from it must be pulled up into the heart. Then the feeling can be put at arms length, seen in a different perspective and released.

Love helps put everything in order. It softens the feeling and degree of intensity. The Universal Creator then easily assists in resolving the situation. Through love, there is surrendering and allowing God to have it. All obstacles seem to move out of the way. The *re-soul-ution* appears.

Once it is explained in this manner, it almost seems too simplistic to be true. Do you remember I spoke earlier about nature being simple? This heart-bridge information on feelings and emotion is the natural way of experiencing life and dealing with actions. Life *can* be that simple.

## Physical Disease from Emotionally Charged Issues

Many people don't know how to regulate feelings through the heart. Sadly, society has not taught the tools needed to direct emotional issues properly. Instead, emotional issues were used to control feelings. As a result, many children become accustomed to an unfeeling atmosphere, laced with only fear, anger, intimidation or unworthiness.

When these feelings are not experienced with love, but encouraged to become emotional, they are pulled too close to the physical body and it becomes manifested as dis-ease.

Feelings are a natural response to the situations in life. It's normal to be angry with someone who pulls his car out in front of you. But when the anger is allowed to build up, then it becomes emotional. It is more difficult to think about it rationally. Soon, rude remarks and judgment cloud the real issue. Negativity is added, and the result of action is lost, or hidden behind emotional energy.

The false emotional energy begins to control the mental, spiritual and eventually the physical body. A large portion of the population is living life through the emotional energy of feelings: Never allowing the element of love to filter the feeling into its proper place. The mind is not able to make rational decisions, the body may become sick due to dis-ease, and the spirit actually is suppressed by muddy auras and unaligned charkas.

After many years of abuse with human feelings, the body, mind and spirit suffer greatly. The physical body must be tended to with holistic practices; the mind has trouble functioning and needs psychological self-help groups to muddle through to the root causes; and, the spirit needs work to rectify all the damages. There is a much better solution: prevention.

The best way to deal with any negative problem is to let the situation just go on by—after the result of action is felt. If it builds up, emotions get in the way. Action is not possible, only re-action. That is loosing control. It gives the power to the emotion.

There are several ways to release the emotions ruling you. This will place the feelings in their proper place.

These emotional cleansing can be facilitated by creative visualization. Eventually, negative emotions can be eliminated from life experience.

1.  Relax and close your eyes. Imagine you are sitting on a beach by the ocean. The waves are rolling in, washing over you and then rolling back to sea.

    As each wave comes to you, see it as a certain upsetting situation experienced recently. The situation washes over you. Acknowledge it, and release it as you see the water go back into the ocean. Do this as many times as needed to really visualize it. Continue experiencing it over again until feel you can release the upsetting situation.

2.  Another visualization to try is this: As you hash over a frustrating day, play a special selection of music. Make sure the tone or rhythm of the music fits the frustration. Start feeling the situation and allow the vibrations of the music to drift the feeling into the heart center. When the music ends, know the frustration is released.

    Every time you think of the frustration, play the music, if needed, and allow it to take the feeling to the correct level. After a period of time, you reprogram the placement of the feeling.

3.  Visualize a cleansing by blowing it in to perspective. Bring back the feeling into your vision. As you think of the pain, take a big breath along with the feeling into your solar plexis for a moment. Then blow the air and the feeling out of your solar plexis, straight up into the feeling body (heart area). There is can commune with the heart and astral body, to evaluate and deal with it.

The best time to do each exercise is just as the situation happens. But if your day is too busy then be sure to take ten minutes out at the end of the day. Do the emotional cleansing techniques with all honesty. Go through the entire day's events and clear all emotional upset from them. The major result is taking control of your life again. Your mind, body and spirit will find new life and vigor.

## Closed Heart Energy

After understanding how important the heart charka is, we can get a look at what is going on with our youth of today. Many children are getting out of control. You hear of children hurting or even killing their parents or other children. Many parents are afraid of their children.

How could this happen? Why are so many children losing direction? Why are they making unwise choices? I believe it to be a situation that has progressed over several generations.

I remember riding in the countryside with our family as a small child. From one end of the county to the other, Dad pointed out different farmhouses. As we passed, he would say he lived in that house when he was a child. After several trips, and several houses, I asked him how he could have lived in all of those houses.

Dad told me about his parents. His father was a tenant farmer. A tenant farmer is a person who works someone else's farmland. They usually get to keep a certain part of the crop for their family's food. And in this case, his family could live in the house on the property.

My dad and his twin brother were the youngest of eight children.

At the time my father was a child, in the early 1900's, money was in short supply. With the depression and the wars, many people had to do whatever they could to make a living.

Grandpa considered himself lucky to be able to earn a living the way he did. He never owned land, and never had a house of his own until after his children were grown and one of them bought him a small farm.

All the children in the family became very ambitious because of their circumstances. They all received some kind of higher education and became professional people. They had the drive to better themselves, financially. They wanted better things and better opportunities for themselves and their children. Thank goodness my family was able to strive for more while still keeping their hearts alive with love and purpose of the Self.

But the early years of the twentieth century were difficult for many people. Many families could have been in the early stages of the closing of heart energy, by becoming disconnected with love and self. Of course, it is perfectly normal and positive for people to want to better themselves. There have been many families able to do that.

The problem comes when finances and outside stimulating forces take precedence over love, morale, honesty and contentment with self. When the need for material things and social status become more important than honoring the purpose of teaching our children love through experience and role modeling, then the direction is not there to guide a young mind.

I'm not talking about forsaking ambition and material things. But it needs to be done with discernment of what is important. To constantly strive for a better life, financially, by disregarding the attention your child's needs, could be instrumental in closing a child's heart. It's never done on purpose. But it happens.

In our world today, many families have both parents working, out of necessity. Single parents work two jobs. Many of us are still feeling the need to strive to better our material lives and ourselves. We feel it important to have outside activities for the kids to stay out of trouble.

Then a disconnection happens within the family by not having enough time to relate as a unit. The media has encouraged society to rush through everything: cooking, dish washing, traveling, and communication. Slowing down for a minute to re-evaluate what we are doing will reveal what is important in life and with family.

When I was a child, my sisters and I had supper with the family every night. We were brought up that way. We sat down at the dinner table. We looked at each other. We talked to each other. Our parents knew how we were doing, because they asked.

This generation is on the run. We don't seem to have time to sit down and eat one meal together. But if we looked at what is really important, maybe we could find the time. Or possibly have family activities during the week.

I have friends who stay in on Tuesday and Thursday evenings. The kids do not have outside activities on those days. They cook together and play a family board game, or work a jigsaw puzzle together. This way, the parents open up a chance for the children to talk about things on their minds.

Their children trust their parents to be there for them when needed. They have a source to go to when they have a question.

Only parents can bring up their child---not outside sources. An outside source only serves as a baby sitter, or pacifier. It can never replace the connection parents have with their children. That connection is love.

They were conceived with love. They were delivered into this world through love. If that connection is not nourished, it dies.

We can keep the heart center open. Our children need to be nurtured. They need to know love. They need us. Then we will have children with their heart centers wide open.

# Chapter 6

# *The Unfoldment Process*

# The Unfoldment Process

*Sitting for Unfoldment (Development)*

Charles and I started going to a spiritualist church in our town, just over 30 years ago. The service was remarkably similar to the Methodist Church I was raised in.

After the main, traditional service there was a Message Service. Different mediums of the church took turns and gave members of the congregation information they received from spirit. This is the main idea behind what is now called Gallery Readings in the secular world.

We found out rather quickly a very strong spiritual community existed in our town. It was not widely advertised. But they remained a close knit group and worked very extensively in outreach activities around town.

I learned to use my intuitive abilities very quickly after joining an unfoldment class there. Every Tuesday night we met in a small dark room with about fifteen other students. We sat quietly in meditation for about an hour. The meditation was followed by sharing feelings or thoughts received during the sitting.

I sat in unfoldment class and practiced in the safe and loving environment of the church for many years. I knew no one would ridicule me for making a mistake because they were all beginners at one time.

I felt comfortable to pursue the practice of working with spirit energies. This is the type of arena you may consider as a comfort zone for unfoldment.

If you and some friends are considering the development of intuition, get together and meet on a regular basis. During the meeting, review the things that interest the group about spirituality. Get to know the other members well. Come to some common ground and understanding. Feel good about each other.

Decide if your group has the kind of spiritual connection to sit for unfoldment together. Unfoldment is allowing the God-given spiritual talents to increase through practice.

Many years after we started going to the spiritualist church in town, we became founding board members of a sister church.

We joined a new unfoldment group there the minister started. There were initially about 12 participants in the group. Everyone was excited about the newness of the unfoldment. We shared our experiences with each other during the class. After about four or five sessions, several of the members dropped out.

Even though they were excited to join the class, they were not ready to commit to the regular sessions. We each have our own comfort zones. Allow differences among your associates and honor those who are on their own path.

Here are a few things useful in opening intuitively:

- Spirituality. It is way of understanding the divine self. Your spiritual awareness comes in the search.

- Dedication is important for unfolding psychic or medium abilities. Any honorable search requires true commitment.

- Meditation is a major tool for unfoldment. Spend time meditating every day to remain open to the inner self.

- Be aware of self and your surroundings. Spend time everyday recognizing the small things at hand.

- Read and research experiences of others. It keeps your mind centered on what you want.

- Share information given to you to gain confidence. Spiritual connections become stronger.

- Become involved in a circle of like-minded people. You will support each other.

- Practice with others who honor and respect the gift. They encourage you and ground your energy.

- Spend time working on exercises to increase potential.

- Take advantage of every workshop, class or lecture beneficial to your craft.

## Levels of Awareness

Everyone has some kind of intuitive ability. Everyone is aware on some level, of spirit; they are aware of those who passed away hovering close by, of impressions of people, places and things. Everyone has feelings about, or knows certain events before they happen.

Becoming intuitively aware is the main reason to develop or unfold. It is for personal, spiritual growth and understanding.

The only reason you may not be aware of things, intuitively, is your life style squeezed intuition out of your awareness. It is still there, but you may be so overcome by your duties in this world, you are not paying attention to the soft murmurs of your inner self.

It is easy to get wrapped up in the physical world. Society has easily stressed the physical and mental make up of this time. As a result, the spiritual aspects to life have been misplaced.

## Body/Mind/Spirit

We as humans live in three different levels: body, mind and spirit. To leave out one section, creates an imbalance. Not having enough time for one means your life is lacking one-third of its existence.

Life is not just the day-to-day events. It is a complex maze of experiences and learning how to deal with them; impressions and expressions; feelings and emotions; physical interactions with people, and making sense of it all.

When born, humans are fully connected with spirit and the inner self. Over the next two-three years young children become de-programmed from the spirit side of life and then re-programmed into the third dimension. Everything known on a soul level is stripped away as they are indoctrinated into the physical dimension of earth.

Parents and loved ones begin their mission to help the child understand what earth is all about. The child becomes more distant from their inner soul understandings. Soon the true self is just a dream or image almost lost in the transition into the physical.

It has been said to weep at a birth and have joy in a death. It must refer to all the misguided although good intentions thrust on a baby. Eventually, the child loses all conscious contact with the strongest energy there is.

Joy at death would refer to flowing back and reuniting with what was known but lost.

Why did we forget? It was only the human thing to do. But now, we realize there is something to remember.

Since we had a mask put over our eyes when we entered this world, we need to take time to re-connect with our spirit selves. That is why it is good to gather friends with like interests to sit for unfoldment. Remember how to be the go-between. You can know your inner self on a more intimate basis, and be aware of the true reality.

## Introduction to Your Inner Being

To accept your Inner Being (or Spirit Being), and realizing a greater, broader perspective is essential to living the joyful, growth-filled physical experience you came here to live.

Without the broader perspective from the inner dimension there is tremendous limitation experienced on the earth. There are constant limits to what you can accomplish by depending on always physically making something happen. In your rush to do things, you become very busy; so busy you forgot the joy in life.

Look at who you are and why you are here in this physical body. Start looking from a bigger perspective to access the joy of life and living, instead of having to always do something.

The desire is always there to understand the connection between the physical you and the inner you. This connection is what makes your life really come alive to fulfill your life-vision.

Think about all the things you did today requiring effort. How many were done without joy? Create a list of meaningless tasks you do on a regular basis that do not serve you.

Resolve to either eliminate one at a time, replacing it with a joy-filled event, or change it in a way to make the task meaningful.

Affirm today, no matter where you go; no matter what you do, it is your most sincere intent to look for all that makes you feel good. Try this short meditation:

> Sit quietly. Be totally aware of your thinking. Be very conscious of your thoughts. Know what it is like to initiate your own thought.

## The Unfoldment Group Experience

When our unfoldment group was together, the minister was the person in control. She said a special prayer of invocation. She sat close to the light switch and closed the door when everyone was there and ready. She stayed awake and conscious during the sessions, to be in charge. She directed the sessions when needed and lead everyone into a meditative state. After about 45 minutes passed by, she brought everyone out of meditation. And they shared experiences.

If you don't have a mediumship or spiritual teacher to assist you in the group, you may choose a different person each time to be in charge of the meeting. It gives everyone a chance to experience leading the session, and can handle it, if necessary.

Everyone will have their share of sitting in meditation. Choose the person the week before, so he can be prepared ahead of time.

Come to the understanding this is an extremely spiritual occasion, with no inconsiderate behavior. Jokes and silly conduct have no place in this setting. However, it is important to keep things upbeat and positive. Light hearted stories and good feelings are very appropriate. It is a coming together to study, experience and learn, not play around.

Agree on a place with a room comfortable for everyone. The view from the windows should be blocked out with heavy curtains or blinds. Disconnect the phone. Ringing phones or loud answering machines can be very disruptive. Do whatever you can to keep the sessions as smooth flowing as possible.

Use the same room every time. Certain energy or vibration is created over a period of time, and it's easier to always be in the same location. Just moving from one place to another makes it difficult to settle down for a peaceful, quiet meditation.

Using a dimmer switch or several candles will allow soft, low lighting. I like the type of light given from a pillar candle. Secure it in a stable container. Beautiful, designer candles have their place, but not in these sessions. Safety is more important.

Incense or some kind of aromatherapy scents can be used if it does not bother anyone. If you decide to study a certain book then make sure everyone has a copy. Or keep inspirational reading materials near the in-charge table.

Other needs or items will come apparent as you progress in the group. It's good to keep things constant, but don't be afraid to change something if it isn't working.

Now sit quietly, and allow spirit to work. Don't try to make anything happen. Just allow. I will be giving exercises later in this section for the group to practice to strengthen intuitive gifts.

## Techniques on Developing Mediumship

To develop mediumship requires time, hard work, study, and patience. It does not manifest after a weekend intensive with certificate of completion.

There is nothing instant about mediumship. Mediumship, intuition and psychic abilities are ongoing processes, requiring considerable practice and study.

Connecting with your first spirit entities or seeing and hearing spirits as a young child is a good starting place. But it does not give the ability to understand how to assist others in dealing with their problems in a reading setting. The responsibility is huge when it comes to this work.

There are many experiences, scenarios and practice for you to do to perfect your newfound ability. It's important to work with a mentor or teacher to recognize what to do in certain situations you have not experienced. Even well established mediums continue to study and be guided, consulting with their teachers on a regular basis.

There are areas to address, helping you know how to present information you receive from spirit. Connecting with a deceased loved one is only the beginning of understanding the process.

Don't be too anxious to hang a reader's sign on your door. Handling certain experiences should be learned in class, not with a live client. It takes fierce responsibility entering someone's personal space.

*Question: I always can receive more psychic information when I'm at a spiritual retreat setting or around a group of highly gifted friends. But when I get back home it's difficult to pick up anything. Why is that?*

*Answer: In places like the spiritual retreat you spoke of, energy is built up over years of spiritual events happening in that specific place. That is why it is appropriate to have unfoldment classes at the same location each time. It sets a special energy field there.*

*Also, when around people who are extremely gifted with high vibrations, you are lifted up to that level. They are virtually giving you a "hand up". When you leave the higher energy field of the retreat, or the company of gifted friends, you return to your normal state of being.*

*To be able to create the high-energy for yourself, so you can benefit from spiritual information as needed, there are several things you can do.*

*In your home create your own sacred space. Meditate there, read spiritually uplifting material there. Listen to high-vibration music or teachings there. Keep the space pure for your spiritual practice only. Do this on a daily basis.*

*This area will continue to grow in higher, finer frequencies. Being in that atmosphere on a regular basis, you will automatically raise your vibrations.*

*When you are out during the day and feel the need to tune into universal knowledge put your being in the sacred space at home…imagine yourself there, or pull the higher sensations around you from that place.*

Before accepting a new mediumship student, I insist the person take a course in Spiritual Counseling, which includes work with meditation, prayer treatment and self-empowerment techniques. This helps round out the individual, creating a strong spiritual base of understanding. If you do not fully understand who you are and what you are studying, it is too easy to be led astray in unfamiliar territory.

Here are more suggestions to start your development in mediumship or psychic abilities:

- The circle should be led by an experienced medium aware of the procedures of unfoldment and development.

- Have at least four people in the circle to hold the energy of your meetings. The combined energy is important. Ten to twelve would be the most to have the time frame needed to share within the group.

- Decide on a day and time everyone will be able to attend on a regular basis. Arrive anywhere from ten to fifteen minutes early to set your mind on what you are there for.

- Try sitting in the same seat each time. The habit you form through timing and arrangement is essential.

- Do not have a large meal just before your session. Your stomach requires a full flow of blood to digest your food. This will take away from your meditation and focus. The same goes for caffeine drinks.

- Always start your sessions with an Opening Prayer of Protection, and some kind of Invocation.

- Start with a development meditation to prepare the connection of communication. This should be at least 10-15 minutes to start, but could stretch to 45 minutes.

- Share messages the students received from spirit or evidence collected during the meditation time. Give everyone allotted time to share messages.

- Prepare an exercise or lesson to stimulate sensitivity and practice within the group.

- Close with a prayer of gratitude or completion so all in the circle are disconnected from their work.

- The length of time for the circle should be from one to one and a half hours. When the work is complete and the circle is closed, everyone should get up and move around. This clears the energy and assists everyone to disconnect from the event.

Mediumship does not happen over night. It takes time to develop and time to understand the complexity of what is happening. Be ready to make a commitment to yourself to work on the gift as long as it takes.

Do not rely solely on the Circle each week to develop your gifts. Study on your own. Read as much as you can to continue your spiritual growth.

*Starting Your Development Meditation*

*As you access or connect the Inner Self with the Outer (physical) Self you expand your understanding. You can intentionally manifest your life experience. Your connection with the Inner Self will be very personalized. But there are certain processes that assist you on your exploration.*

*The Inner Self. Your Spirit constantly shares knowledge with your conscious self. Be available to access the pathway of connection.*

*Desire. Desire to open the pathway is important for the process to happen. As long as you desire it and work towards the opening on a consistent basis, you will succeed.*

*Finding Time. Fifteen to twenty minutes each day is good. Be consistent in the habit of sitting for opening.*

*Be Still and Quiet. Allow your conscious mind to rest. Be still and quiet without thinking on purpose about anything. At first your ego mind will want to be in control.*

*Your Intention. As you sit to quiet your mind, the physical body starts to relax. The mind will also release stress. You feel very relaxed; possibly ready to sleep. But your intention is to sit for development and opening to the Inner Self. Stay awake and conscious of your experience.*

*Numb Feeling. Your body will start to feel different, sluggish or stiff. It may seem numb or separate from you. This alignment opens your pathway to spiritual awareness. At this point just allow the process to take place.*

*Fully Engaged. Soon after sitting regularly, different parts of the body (fingers, head or torso) will move without you purposely making it move. This is when your Inner Self is fully engaged. The Inner Spirit is actively conducting the music now. Just enjoy the tune and know full communication is taking place.*

*Alignment. The alignment of Spirit and the Outer Self can only be done during this opening of the pathway. You are not able to achieve it on your own, consciously. So there is no need to try to do it. Just allow it.*

## Communication Between Two Worlds

The main purpose of communicating between the two worlds is to receive impressions of love and truth from those in the spirit world.

Truth is a spiritual law. You must prepare yourself physically, mentally and spiritually to understand the information that comes from the spirit realm.

Following in a spiritual path makes you stronger than you can imagine. The strength is in body, mind and spirit. By honoring yourself as all three aspects of being you become a whole person.

## True Spirit Communication

Sit for a period of 15-20 minutes clearing your mind of superficial self-talk. Focus on your breathing and allow the pathway between your conscious self and spirit self to open.

After you recognize your body is moving with out your conscious request, you are truly in the communication mode with your inner being. The alignment has taken place. Communication is activated, but still in a primitive stage.

If you sit for the 15-20 minutes or less, and receive the movement response, you are ready for the next phase. Here are some things to remember:

- When you want communication from your Higher Self, or Spirit, be sure to have a question ready, or at least a general idea or topic. It must always be a rewarding and uplifting session; it is for your edification.

- Spend some time really deciding what you will ask. Be very specific. Your answer will only be as specific as your question

- Quiet your mind as usual for the communication, but remain conscious to understand the answer coming to you. It probably will not be words delivered to you from your Higher Self. It will be ideas, or a "knowing". Try hearing with your mind and heart instead of your outer ears. Expect it to take awhile to get a feel for it.

- It usually takes a few seconds for the idea to be presented and the conscious mind to translate it into physical words. Do not get frustrated, but allow the process to take as long as needed.

- Your first attempts will feel awkward and slow. It will be similar in learning to ride a bike. Many mistakes will happen, but that is the process of learning.

- After you pose your question, separate your thoughts from question mode into receiving mode by taking a few deep breaths. Then wait for the slightest impulse or fleeting thought to enter your mind.

You will probably second-guess yourself as to whether it is an answer from the Higher Self or from your own conscious thoughts. This is normal. After awhile, you may notice a subtle difference between the two. Generally, your own thoughts may flit around from one thing to another. But information from Spirit will be smoother and actually feel rhythmical.

If your own thoughts are getting in the way of communication, you may feel uneasy or begin to doubt what you are getting.

You should stop the session and try again another time. By continuing in doubt, you only welcome in lower energies that like to trick or confuse.

The next time you start a communication session, be sure to have a clear intent on the question, open to the possibility of connecting to higher vibrations and the communication will be good.

After continued practice, you will connect much easier and it will be a very special relationship. You will have a broader view of the world and all things that affect you in it.

You now become much more familiar with your Guidance System. It puts you on the path of your spiritual growth, and allows you to become and know the things you originally set out to accomplish in this physical lifetime.

## Go Slowly

In the early stages of your unfoldment, be very cautious whenever you receive information that seems to be of spirit. It may be just that, but may not be. It is time to question everything and expect to be given proof of some kind to be convinced of the true nature of the information.

This is the first area of discerning of spirit. If you were to accept everything that seems to be from your guides, you will believe anything. You could be led astray easily because of it. It's better to question to a fault, than to be taken advantage of later by a malevolent energy.

When a person dies and regains full residence in the spirit world, does not give him "all-knowing".

He does not have any higher knowing (in most cases) than he did just before he passed away. Take any information from that spirit as common knowledge and not a directive for your life.

During these early times of development, be wary of spirits giving the name of a well known or highly evolved entity. More common than not, if a highly evolved entity does work with you, he will probably never tell you who he is. Most teachers or spirit doctors do not find it important to reveal who they are. It actually detracts from the information given.

By all means, take your time while on this journey. It is the learning over time that is important. Time and experience transform a good medium into a medium of high integrity.

## *Working with Guides*

You have a whole community of spirit guides around you to see you through life. Guiding forces have been part of our existence since the beginning of time.

Usually, your guides will present themselves in human form, or with a familiar name. Historically, a guide will be of a special culture or ethnic origin, such as Native American, Chinese, Egyptian, Irish, etc.

Your guide may have a certain vocational association: physician, musician, professor, healer, etc. Others may present themselves as a color, sound or sensation like royal blue, chimes, north wind.

The main reason for this is so to associate with the guiding force in an easier manner. Many people feel more comfortable with the idea of Inner Self or Higher Self. These are wonderful ways of looking at it.

There are three general classifications of guides:

1. <u>Personal Guides.</u> These guiding forces are around you all
   your life. It is their mission to assist you in any way
   needed. They gently nudge you into positive situations.
   But we don't always pay attention at the time. You may
   be attracted to something that represents your guide. This
   could be a flower, or a rainbow, or a crystal, for example.

2. <u>Guides for Special Gifts or Talents</u>. These guides may be
   with you all your life, or only a short period of time.
   Their main purpose is to help you in an area of expertise,
   such as, playing the piano, a knack for working with
   children, or weaving a blanket.

3. <u>Master Teacher or Doctor</u>. These guides are specifically
   for your spiritual growth. Many of them help in healing
   techniques or spiritual counseling. They may also help
   you in communicating with people or teaching.

Before spirit incarnated into the bodies we have now, we decided
the experiences we wanted to help our soul evolve. After taking
on the physical body, we may be doing other things than our life
purpose.

This is when your guide will come to influence you and gently
urge you onto the path again. He will never tell you what to do or
make you do something against your nature. The guide is only
there to assist you. You always have free will, and can choose to
follow the advice or not.

Sometimes loved ones you knew in this lifetime may come to
help you. Even though your loved one comes with love and help,
the advice she has may not always be helpful. You may have
taken Aunt Sue's advice when you were 10 years old.

She is still operating with the same mental capacity. Her spirit has not evolved as greatly as your spirit guides have.

Being in the spirit world does not guarantee enlightenment. Better to seek the advice or counsel of a more evolved guide or spirit who can give you a broader look at the problem, rather than a limited earthly view. Then you can embrace Aunt Sue for encouragement on the path.

Who are your spirit guides?

I have a very personal opinion of who spirit guides generally are. This is not something any one told me, nor have I learned it in any seminars or classes. It is information brought through spirit in many different readings I have given and other meditative moments.

I believe guiding spirits are representations of previous lives. Imagine a large wagon wheel. The center cog of the wheel represents your life now. This is the one small part of yourself you are right now. The outer wheel represents all you have ever been. And the spokes are different interpretations of lifetimes you have experienced.

As you live this present life, you may need help in familiar areas or experiences. Then a past life remembrance is made known to you in the form of a guiding spirit.

The essence or spirit of a previous life is always connected to the soul. When the soul realizes you need guidance it provides you with a past life experience through the system of spirit guides.

These guides are usually with you for the whole lifetime. It is easier for humans to grasp the idea of help coming from individual beings, than to imagine it as an essence, energy or vibration. It's easier to describe this as a spirit guide.

Reincarnation fits in here, of course.

A client of mine asked if her grandmother who was gone over ten years was all right. Immediately, I connected with grandmother's spirit energy through my spirit doctor. I described her in detail including personality traits and information for the family.

Then an unusual thing happened. To my surprise, I told her grandmother already reincarnated. The client asked the obvious question: "If grandma already reincarnated, how can you talk to her?" She wouldn't be in the spirit world, would she?

Amazing information was made available: something I was never taught in the spiritual classes I had attended.

The essence or memory of the loved one who passed over is energy with a special imprint. This imprinted energy is like a grid of information representing the loved one (grandma). The medium connects with this representation. We can connect with this memory even though the soul has reincarnated another life.

It's like being in two places at the same time. Grandmother's essence was already a guiding spirit for the newly incarnated human being. In other words, the soul-group the grandmother belonged to reincarnated another spirit. And the essence (grandmother) was helping the new life as a guide.

As I look back at being a young girl, iris flowers were always my favorite. My mother took great pride in her flower gardens. Many of them were irises.

I usually picked as many as my hands would hold and present them as a gift to Mom. The beautiful periwinkle color was an exciting color for me.

Pictures in the magazines we got at home with irises in them always drew my attention. I just thought I had affection for irises.

After I started sitting in unfoldment class the first time, I began to wonder if I had a spirit guide represented by an iris. Sometimes other mediums would tell me the names of my guides, but never by the name of Iris.

I wanted to find out for myself. Sometimes it is better to know something under your own power than from outside means.

One evening while sitting quietly in meditation at home, I sincerely asked if I had a guiding force around me known as Iris, it would be made apparent to me. I asked to be given a very physical, material clue so there was no doubt in my mind. Then I let it go and forgot about it.

My sister called the next day. Our cousin, who owned a small gift shop, was having an open house. She thought we should go. While we were there, we filled out small papers with name, address and phone number for a door prize. We didn't see what the prizes were; we just wanted to be on her mailing list.

Two days went by and my cousin called to congratulate me. I had won the first prize in the give away. How great! "What is it?" I asked.

"It's a beautiful craved wood wall hanging. Come in and pick it up."

So I did. Guess what was carved on it? A picture of a wild iris flower!

All those years I was attracted to the iris, but only then did I fully understand what it meant.

Be very aware of your surroundings. If there seems to be a special connection to you ask for confirmation.

I see this as being in the zone, or the field of synchronicity. When things of like vibration seem to catch your attention, it is important to pay attention to them and find out what the meaning is for you.

## *Astral Level:*
## *Departed Loved Ones and Other Spirits*

There is a realm or dimensional area just beyond our third dimension. Of course, we live physically in the third dimension. After we leave the body through physical death, our spirit merges fully into the next dimension. It is called the Astral Realm. Some believe the spirit actually lives in the astral while inhabiting the physical body or dimension.

The astral plane is where all spirits go after the so-called death occurs. If we are spiritually aware to any extent, while still in the living, we come to a greater awareness, after death, and move into the higher end of that dimension or beyond. However, most deceased loved ones are in the astral.

By all accounts, the astral is not a very evolved area. It is simply a place that enables us to stay close to the physical world we have grown so accustomed to. Perhaps your husband, wife or children are still living. The attachment is so strong you can't seem to pull away from it.

Many have spent a lifetime amassing wealth, and will never leave it. Not even after death. Alcoholics, who frequented bars every night during life, still frequent the bars while in the spirit.

They are drawn to people who are living the same type of life they did.

The same holds true for hardened criminals. They tend to gravitate to people who are continuing in the same life experience the criminal spirit remembers.

This information gives us a chance to look at spirit communication a little differently. It's easier to realize not all spirit entities are the best to commune with. Being in contact with a spirit requires discernment as to the level of their understanding. The information that comes through will tell of their awareness of spiritual matters and intentions.

A loving, strongly evolved spirit or guide would never speak badly of anyone. They would never ask you to say something to embarrass anyone. It would never ask you to do something against your nature. If this is the kind of spirit that is communicating with you, you need to re-evaluate who you are receiving messages from. They are not of good intention.

If you are not comfortable with the information given to you, do not accept it. Tell the spirit to move away from you, and leave you alone. Then reassess your guiding circle. Ask for the most spiritually evolved guides and angels to assist you. You may have to re-learn a new way of communicating or working with spirit.

## *Receiving and Delivering from Spirit.*

As I continued my education and experiences in working closely with the spirit realm, I came to appreciate those who assisted me in my endeavors. They are the angels, master teachers and guides who were close to me.

I was able to connect with energies I needed, to find out information for someone or connect with a departed loved one for a client.

I learned very early not to go looking for the loved ones on my own. I direct my spirit doctor to find them and funnel information to me. That way, I am not directly connected to any emotional upsets or traumas in their vibration. There is nothing wrong with the vibrations they carry. However, I am interested in the information, not the sensationalism connected with it.

If I get too caught up with the emotion, or erratic vibration, it lingers with me long after the spirit is gone.

I prefer to work in a more disconnected manner. That way, I can remain in charge, and control the manner in which we proceed.

I know there is sensationalism when it comes to spirit communication. I have seen what happens to mediums when they allow themselves to be used in that way.

Being open to spirit energy more than normal, they are constantly vulnerable to inconsistent and unknown energy and vibration. As a result, their auras have holes in them which result in illness. I have seen many mediums die in their early 50's because of this constant connection with spirits.

I choose to be more guarded. By using my guides as mediators (between me and the spirit-beings in question) I am always receiving the vibration in a consistent manner and never shifted between varying spirit frequencies. It is a steady flow and I know where my point of connection is: the guide I have worked with for so many years, who I trust.

## Exercises to Help Unfoldment

The world of spirit is different than our physical world. Communicating with spirit requires adjustment. When evolved spirits reach through to our world, it is done purely with love. It needs to be fine tuned or compacted in some way. At the same time, you must raise yourself to the highest level of love vibration possible.

Many spirits exist in the astral dimension, which is the next level of understanding from our own. This is where many deceased loved ones radiate. The master guiding forces you want to commune with are on the Mental and possibly Causal Planes. Focus your intention there. More information is in the chapter "How You Can Talk to Heaven and How You Can't".

### Exercise #1
### Visualization through Love: The Light of Spirit

The best way I found to raise your vibrations is to use the Light of Spirit Visualization.

> Sit quietly and bring your breath to an even flow. As you sit comfortably, imagine the flame of a small candle.
>
> Concentrate on the vision of the flame in your mind. As you connect with the vision and can hold it, see the flame situated inside your heart where love springs forth. This light represents the love of the world. Just see the flame inside your heart center.
>
> The more you sit with the light inside you, the easier it becomes to continue with the vision. Soon the flame begins to glow and grow fuller. See it gets bigger. As the flame grows larger, so does the love vibration. It has a wonderfully warm feeling.

As you breathe, the flame gets bigger. Little by little, it starts to seep through your being, through your skin and body and radiates all around you.

As it grows, it covers your entire body and feels like a large spot light shining on you. But it is not an external light. It is the light of love within.

The light continues to grow. The larger it becomes and the farther it reaches from you, the easier it is for the spirit guides to connect with you.

After several sessions of this visualization, it will become automatic for your light to shine. The spirit connection will happen spontaneously.

*Slow Down the Mind*

You are on a search for Truth. That is your fundamental purpose in Life. You may spend your whole life trying to figure out what truth really is.

Life's unimportant things try to distract you from it. Your mind will attach importance to these barriers and you will be led to believe they are truth. Realize truth comes from your Inner Self.

It's time to identify and break down those barriers. They should be honored, because they are a part of you. But they should be put into their proper places.

## Exercise #2
## Remembering the Closeness of Creator

This exercise is a very simple one. It may so simple you don't recognize how powerful it can be. Remember I said natural and simple is always better?

Pay attention to nature to recognize the Creator Source, God. Harmony is in every aspect of nature. By focusing on these natural forces, you are more attuned to the Higher Vibrations.

Being attuned to the Higher Vibrations, your vibrations are raised too.

**Examples of becoming harmonious to life:**
~~Pick up the brown earth to connect to Mother Earth and the marvels of nature. Smell the sweetness of earth.
~~Smell the new mowed lawn.
~~Enjoy the falling rain instead of feeling irritated with it
~~Appreciate the artistic value of a flower or leaf

## Connection and Ego

Over several months of sitting in my first unfoldment class, in 1980, I remembered I already knew how to commune with spirit. As I sat in class one evening, a passing thought flowed through my mind. I saw a soft breezy meadow. The grass was high. An old milk cow grazed, and two small children ran toward it. They were playing but had a purpose in running towards the cow. I thought it was a daydream.

When the meditation was over, our minister asked us all to describe anything we heard, saw or felt. We each took turns. When it was my turn, I told about a cold chill I experienced. I saw whirling blue and yellow colors. That was all. I didn't mention the daydream.

"You didn't see anything else?" he asked. No was my answer. Then I remembered the daydream.

"Well, I did see a cow in a meadow…" and I continued to describe the scene. As it turned out the minister and his sister used to run out to the meadow to bring in the old cow their family owned. It was their job when they were young.

His sister passed away years before. She was showing me something in my daydream. It was coming from his vibration. But it seemed like a memory to me.

The first few times it happened that way, I dismissed it as imagination. Slowly I realized I have always received information from spirit. Imagination and creative visualization is the same thing. This is how spirit can present things---through the inner vision.

On another occasion, I told about an older man I saw with another member of the class. I told every detail, including a very large nose, as represented by Jimmy Durante (an entertainer from the 1950's). That was a figure in my memory that my psychic eye, or inner vision could show me. She said it was her father, in spirit.

Finally I got it. It is a thought appearing in the mind. It seems like imagination. Sometimes it comes when you least expect it.

Sometimes it comes when you ask. The main thing is to be aware. Test what you think is information from spirit. You will know if it is your thought or that of spirit. If you doubt the information and believe it could only be your own thoughts, it probably is.

If the information is a confirmation to something you already know and may add extra wisdom to the area, it is from a higher source. If it comes in a smooth and unencumbered way, then it usually is from your guidance system.

Slowly but surely I kept progressing. Soon I was presenting during the message service at church. Every last Sunday of the month all the students had a chance to practice sharing messages with the congregation.

I was working with psychometry, holding an object that belonged to someone. After becoming sensitive enough, you can feel or sense certain things about the owner or where the object had been. (More about psychometry later in this chapter)

The usher went through the congregation with a basket to collect watches, keys and other objects from willing participants.

I stood behind the lectern. The basket was in front of me. I took a cross out of the basket, and held it up. A man in the back of the church recognized it. I closed my eyes and held the cross in my hands. Immediately I saw an airplane, and said so.

He said, "Yes that's right."

I elaborated, "Not just an airplane, but a bi-plane---with layered wings."

He said, "Yes, I know what you're talking about."

I was so ecstatic I almost jumped up and down. I was so proud of myself. I assumed it was all I was getting and went on to the next object. I continued quickly with small visions of things or words or colors. Soon it was time for the next person to practice.

Later that day, I had time to reflect on the message service, and how well it went. Then, like a toy boat that had broken loose from the river moss, more information came rushing through about the bi-plane.

The man was looking for an answer concerning the operation of the plane. What he was looking for was behind the instrument panel. I didn't give spirit a chance to relay the information to him. I was too concerned with the *excitement* of the message. I blocked the rest of the information from coming through. I didn't let it flow.

That is what I've stated before about the *sensationalism* of mediumship. The years of needing evidence are very rapidly closing. Most people of the world need more detailed information about their lives and their circumstances. The evidence of the spirit world is already established. Now we need spiritual leaders to take everyone a step forward in the evolution of mankind. It's time to open our hearts and look for more.

*Do not assume your client only wants to be entertained or amazed. Give them the full measure of the connection you hold for them.*

My clients are now looking for their life path. Many are quitting their mundane jobs and dedicating themselves to work with humanity. They already know their loved ones are all right. They are past eating milk toast. They need more substantial food for their souls. Our consultations and counseling sessions are to uplift and empower.

The man I gave the message to was a visitor to the church, and I had no way of getting in touch with him, to share the rest of the message. I learned a lot that day. NEVER let ego get in the way. There is no room for ego in spiritual endeavors. It does not help anyone. It only gets in the way and blocks you from the full truth.

If you are spiritually given a message, don't accept it as all the information. Ask if there is more! More will be given, if it is needed.

Sometimes the verification of an object, like the bi-plane, is the only important thing. But sometimes, the object leads to more meaningful information.

As the years of being a student medium went by, I realized I had been doing this all my life. It took the unfoldment classes to give me a chance to recognize it and learn how to use it properly.

I was given all kinds of information in my younger years (as you may have also experienced), but thought it was just imagination.

## *UltraSense™*

Sense is the ability to perceive something, in what ever way available. To perceive our environment we have five senses: seeing, hearing, tasting, smelling and touching. All of these senses are normal or average to each individual, generally speaking. In this case, all these senses are recognized in a physical way.

Each sense takes on a physical aspect of recognition. To see something, it is physically experienced with the eyes. Hearing is experienced physically with the ears. Taste is physically experienced with the tongue. Smell is physically experienced with the nostrils and touch through the skin.

This is something normally understood and accepted. We are physical beings, so it makes sense to perceive in a physical way.

Now look at this a bit further. Ultra means beyond what is average. We all have five ultra senses complimenting our regular senses. They are enhanced to such a degree they are perceived in the spirit realm or dimension (which is beyond the third dimension or physical reality).

They are presented in a spiritual vibration. Not only are we physical beings, we are also spiritual beings and sense things in a spiritual way.

I prefer the word ultra instead of the word super. If we called it super senses, it would be looked at as something better than normal. In reality, it is only an expanded version of the physical senses. It is a deeper awareness.

You may recognize the term clairvoyance. It means clear sight. It would actually be better to say sight more deeply perceived in a finer vibration. Clairvoyance is known as seeing in a spiritual way rather than a physical way. This would be as picturing in the mind rather than in the brain.

Picturing in the mind is brought about in the same way as imagination. It is possible to see your front door in your mind, because you have memory of it stored there. Since the mind is the bridge between the soul and the brain, it is possible to see other things in the mind.

When a person thinks of something earnestly, he creates mental images and manifests his thought into form on the spiritual realm. Some clairvoyants can read that mind image.

Those who exist in the spiritual world create thought forms as well, and mediums can read those thoughts in the same way. Some mediums see a picture of how a person looked when he was alive. But others can see the entity as a living spirit.

Clairaudience is ultra hearing. It is sound heard in the mind. This could be music, whistles or words. It is similar to talking to yourself in your mind.

There is a fine line between your words (from the ego part) and that given through your inner self (spirit).

Once you become aware of hearing clairaudiently, be wary of astral-level garbage. There is clutter noise and trivia in the astral. You can be overwhelmed by it, and very impressed with all the connections you can make there. But it all is of no consequence, only confusing information. It sometimes takes awhile to sift through the different conditions and feel comfortable with an evolved area of spiritual information.

This information can be from spirit helpers or telepathic messages from people still in the flesh. Discernment is needed in hearing clairaudiently. It helps determine whether it is from spiritual or physical means. One is not better that another, only different. It is important to be able to distinguish the difference.

Clairsentience is the ultra perception of touch. We physically touch to experience tactilely, which can give us added information. But just as in a heart-touching experience, ultra touch is dealing with the extended sense of discernment or feeling a sensation. It can be responding to stimulation mentally rather than physically: sensing danger, or negative vibrations, for example.

As you become aware of clairsentience, you can recognize the impression of a new career opportunity or the way a child misses his father. These things come as impressions, sensations or feelings. It can also be called "just knowing".

The same is true for smelling and tasting, although these senses are not as commonly realized. They don't initially make as much of an impression as the first three mentioned: Although the UltraSenses of taste and smell can be just as powerful.

But once you get a spiritual whiff of grandmother's talcum powder after she's been gone for five years, there is no mistaking who is around you.

## Symbols-The Language of Spirit

Let's take a look at the use of symbols in your unfoldment. I call it the Language of Spirit because it is the easiest and fastest way for your guiding forces to connect with you and give you information you will recognize.

The foundation starts in such a simple way: experiences, especially experiences of your early childhood.

### Mind-Brain Connection

Your brain and your mind are two completely different things. The brain is a physical part of the body. The mind is something apart from and beyond the body. The mind taps into the brain for power and connects the spirit to the physical.

Our consciousness is divided into two parts:

1.  The Waking Conscious Mind. This deals with the here and now, and makes decisions. This is the rational part of ourselves with logical thinking.

2.  The Subconscious Mind. The subconscious is in two parts: (A) The personal aspect of the subconscious, and (B) the far deeper and more extensive level, which we share with all sentient life.

    If you have read any works by U. S. Andersen, you will recognize the subconscious as the Universal Mind. Dr. Carl Jung describes it as the Collective Unconscious.

If you consider these two aspects of the mind, psychic development consists of building up certain links between the normal waking consciousness and the subconscious.

After years of acknowledging only the conscious mind, a barrier has been made between the two.

The link which psychic development forms has to pass through this barrier. The result of inner clairvoyant perception moves up into the waking conscious. Traditional thought maintains there is only one sense of psychic perception. But these results come through in various ways.

Just as basic physical senses have several divisions, so does the psychic faculty of perception.

Clairvoyance, clairaudience, and clairsentience are divisions of expression for the one basic psychic perception.

Conscious mind is the here and now, it makes decisions. The subconscious supervises the body's functions. Under perfect conditions this happens without your knowledge and all is well.

Another function of the subconscious is it stores away any information you get through your conscious mind.

This information can be brought back again for future use. The stronger the connection is made with the information, the easier it is for your subconscious to bring it back to the conscious mind. Every word you have ever read, every pothole you have run over, every boring detail, as well as the exciting ones, is stored there.

The subconscious doesn't bring back everything---only the things you access. It creates a well-worn path to the conscious mind and is easy to bring back. If there's a new book you've read, and you tell three people the author's name, the name will stick with you quicker than the author of your biology text in high school. The only reason you can't bring up information quickly is you haven't recalled it enough to create a strong link. The pathway is overgrown and not well worn.

It's important to realize you can still access the information about the biology author. However, your subconscious mind has to spend more time researching and remembering where the information is stored.

Your divine file clerk (subconscious mind) looks in the file marked Biology. After much time, he realizes it is not there.

He then looks in the file marked High School. More time goes by and he can't find it there.

Then subconscious mind looks in the file marked Authors. Nope, he can't find it there, either.

Finally, your subconscious mind finds the author of the biology book in the file marked Boring Information. This is the largest file in your subconscious, and since the detail has not been used much, it takes longer to access.

Symbols in your life experience work the same way.

The universe experiences through your life, so every experience is there in the universal mind of God. This keeps you connected to your spirit. There would be no reason for you to be here in the flesh if your spirit did not want to have experiences. You're here to experience the physical third dimensional world to add to the vast knowledge of the universe.

Every time you cross the street, read a book, get in your car, or argue with your parents, you are making your connection stronger. You are also making memories.

God experiences life through our experiences. We are all part of the whole, the universal oneness. Being spirit, you chose to come to the third dimension to experience and send back your experiences to expand the wisdom of the Universe.

Your mind is activated by the energy of spirit. That, in turn energizes the brain. The only reason you retain memory is this: your brain is activated to be the vehicle of the mind. When my physical body dies, Melissa's body can't recall any information. But the spirit of Melissa has every bit of information she experienced.

That is the main reason intuitives and mediums can contact the information. It is now in the Universal Mind. Many believe mediums only talk to the dead. Well, a medium is a connection between the physical and the spirit, also known as the go-between.

Of course, mediums contact the spirit of people how have died, but they also can contact the spirit of someone still living. It's the energy field or aura of the spirit around the physical that is tapped.

Every experience in your life is registered in your subconscious mind. These experiences are remembered by thinking of certain items, words, people or places. There is a thing or person that will remind you of an event.

When you start talking about the game of Monopoly, each person around you will have a different memory.

In much the same way, your subconscious mind holds meanings. All you have to do is trigger these meanings. This is where symbols come in. They are your memory enhancers.

*Perspective*
Thousands of years in the future, archeologists will unearth ancient burial crypts and sacred inner sanctums. They will find special buildings designated for ceremonial burials. They will find lavish entrances requiring special keys to gain access. The floors will be of marble and lush carpets.

The lighting will be from intricately cut crystals. And there will be guards entombed to protect the noted occupants.

There are different areas or compartments for distinguished citizens and their families, each member having their own chamber. The bodies are be draped with the same type of flowing garments, denoting the levels for their honorable families.

In each compartment there will be a kind of sanctuary for each family to worship their god. It will have luxurious fabrics gracing the walls and many sacred triangle symbols all around.

The compartment has special seating and an enclosed pool for sacraments or baptisms. Do you recognize this ancient burial ground?

Remember I said it would be thousands of years in the future they find these ruins? It actually is not burial crypt. It is a hotel building after a natural disaster.

The compartments are the individual hotel rooms. Each body was simply lying in bed during the disaster; the sanctuary is really the bathroom with curtains hanging around the bathtub (for baptisms) and the symbolic triangles were on the end of fresh towels and bathroom tissue denoting the quarters were recently cleaned by the maid.

Thousands of years from now, the people living in that time may not know anything about hotels. They only understand what they find as it is associated with something they recognize: Something from their own frame of reference, or perspective.

It is with your perspective that you understand something. If your guide sends you a symbol from your memory, it means what you remember by it.

There are books that describe symbols. Certain esoteric symbols have established meanings. They may be the historic meaning, but if your memory brings a different meaning, then honor that.

Many people believe the symbol of the serpent or snake means something evil, because of established long-term use. But to my memory it means full spiritual knowledge. So when I see a snake in a client's vibrations during a consultation, I know they are becoming divinely inspired with information.

Sometimes an apple may be well known for knowledge. But if the vision of an apple reminds you of spending time with your grandfather in his apple orchard, honor that meaning.

The symbol is being brought back in your consciousness through your subconscious, as a way of your guides connecting with you and bringing you information.

Just remember your symbols are very special to you. They can be personal messages given to you or to someone near you.

There are several kinds of symbols that arise in the mind:

- There are symbols that arise in dreams. These are mainly concerned with your internal mental states, but occasionally they are psychic impressions coming into your conscious awareness. The study and manipulation of the dream symbols is a major part of what psychologists and psychiatrists are involved in.

- There are other symbols that have gown up in a haphazard fashion within your mind. When your clairvoyance begins to develop, it will use these symbols.

It is possible for you to build up a planned and selected code of symbols to persuade your psychic faculties to use.

If you decide to work with this, be prepared for resistance from your subconscious when you start. It will usually prefer its own haphazard, homemade code.

It's important to train your conscious mind to respond to those psychic impressions you have formed from infancy. That way, you will be in control of them instead of your subconscious being in control. Most of those impressions were locked in your subconscious because you were taught very early it was not real, only imagination.

Imagination helps a child keep contact with the spiritual side of life. With out imagination, all memory of communication can be lost. A child's imagination is the link to his full psychic development.

You will grow to accept these impressions and make vast growth in your psychic ability. They probably will come randomly, or when you least expect it.

In order to control the flourishing intuition, and start receiving it when you ask for it, practice this exercise regularly with a friend or in your weekly unfoldment circle.

> Get situated in your seat and ease into a quiet space. Spend a few minutes concentrating on your breathing. Have your friend (or the person in charge of the circle) read these instructions to you:
>
> "I will be giving you a word. When I say this word, you should ask your subconscious to bring a memory that corresponds to the word.
>
> "An example of this would be as follows: the word is *feather*. You may have this instant impression of a ticklish situation.

Another may think of proud as a peacock, in association with the feather. Ask for a memory to bring the meaning of the word I give you. Then ask your spirit guides or true self to always use these words as symbols that represent memories."

Below you will find a list of symbols to start with. I've added a space after each word for you to add the meaning you connect with.

It's especially good to practice and experiment with the use of these words together in your development group. It builds confidence. Sharing your information with each other helps to solidify it into your mind.

Here are the words:

Boxes _____

Book _____

Doorway _____

Trash _____

Crossroads _____

Heart _____

Dove _____

Tree _____

You may add to the list of symbols, but go slowly so you have a chance to incorporate them. If you go too fast, you won't spend enough time with the memories to keep the association.

Memorize these symbols and their memory-meanings. They will be a major part of your clairvoyant messages. Other impressions, feelings, sounds and statements may begin to come along with each symbol.

Continually tell your subconscious mind every time you receive a message these special symbols will be used. Do that with each symbol.

While receiving information intuitively, the symbols will always mean what you agreed on. I have found it is very important to say what the symbol is to the person you are working with first before identifying what it means in  your experience.

After you make progress with this exercise, turn it around. Make a list of concepts or feelings you want to have symbols for. Your subconscious will be used to the exercises and give you great symbols.

One particular consultation I gave several years ago comes to my mind as an example. I was called by Nancy, who I had met while exhibiting at a Noetic Science Conference. She received a consultation from me at that time. About seven months later she called to receive a phone session from me.

As I first connected with her vibrations, I saw dandelions. Even though the symbol was directed from her vibrations, my guide gave it to me through my subconscious. My memory of dandelions was of health-related purposes and spring tonics. Before I told her the meaning, I first told her the symbol I saw. "I see dandelions in your vibrations."

She burst out in laughter. "You really see dandelions? She replied, still laughing.

"Yes, I see a field of dandelions," and I continued to tell her the meaning behind it, from my perspective. It had to do with nature and herbal cures. By the time I finished, she was still laughing. Some people might feel intimidated by this, but I simply asked why she was laughing.

"Just before I called you for the session, I brewed myself a cup of dandelion tea. I'm sipping on it right now."

Nancy also explained her family always went out in the spring to gather dandelion greens to cook. It had become a family tradition.

This happens quite often. The object you see will actually represent something literally in the client's life, besides having a symbolic meaning.

Be ready for anything. If you see something not in your personal list of symbols, it usually means something literal. But be open for anything.

As soon as you say what the item is, your guiding forces may give you more information about it. Sometimes it is so intense the new symbol will become one of your own.

*Building a bridge:*
This exercise builds a bridge between the conscious and subconscious, between the brain and the mind. You will be much more in control of your power to receive. The random acts of homemade symbols will fade and a stronger sense of understanding will come. You have informed your subconscious mind what you expect of it.

As this form of exercise continues, you will become more familiar with the technique and more confident with the skill.

The use of your personal symbols will be a great foundation to your growth and development. Your guides will be able to connect with you through this foundation and build a great relationship. The use of symbols is just a starting place. Much more will come after you are confident in what you are receiving.

## *Psychometry*

Psychometry is psychic measuring. It detects or discerns the auric emanations surrounding and contained in different objects. You can detect information on where the object has been or about the person who has owned it.

> *Exercise:* Put these items in a box or basket: rocks, crystals, tree bark, fabric, tissue paper, plastic, or an assortment of different inanimate objects. Everything in the universe has a vibratory rate: animate and inanimate. That is what creates it into a   manifested form. Denser objects have slower, heavier vibrations. Thinner, softer or more porous objects have a faster or higher vibration.
>
> Clear your mind and take an item out. Hold it in your hand and sense what it is and where it came from. The feeling you are looking for is not a tactile feeling, but a sense or impression.
>
> Go with your first impressions. Many tradesmen, craftsmen and artists have developed this high rate of sensitivity. Become aware of the different vibrations, special feelings and impressions. They are very subtle at first. So if you think you feel something then you do. Just say it.

This can be practiced at home during your meditative times or with the unfoldment group. If you are doing it in a group setting, take turns with the basket. This way, you will learn so much more through others experiences.

After you are feeling confident with this practice, start using objects that belong to the class members. The best objects are always something made of metal, such as keys, rings, watches. But you already know other things have vibrations, so a tube of lipstick or handkerchief will work too.

The person "reading" the object should stand up and walk over to the person he is working with. Stand in front of that person but DO NOT take anything yet.

Greet that person in some way (Good Evening, or What's your name?). Making eye contact is always proper for positive connection and respect.

Close your eyes and take a deep, clearing breath. Ground yourself in some way. See your feet in the ground or be fully in the body. Then extend your hand for the object.

As soon as you get the object in your hand, start talking. Say everything you see, feel or hear. When using psychometry, do not hesitate. There is no need to think or concentrate long. That could block the information. The secret is to just blurt it out.

If what you receive does not make sense to you, do not ask the client what it means. It's always best to not ask your clients questions that may be fed back to them later. Ask your guides for more information.

The best way to know about information that is unclear is to ask. This will actually help your unfoldment process grow and the connection with your guides and higher self become stronger.

After you have received the information, say what you have, no matter how strange it might seem. Then, after you have said it, you may ask your client if they understand what it is.

Practice with different articles as much as possible. If you have trouble at first receiving information, then imagine something in your mind's eye. (For instance, if you were getting information, what would it be? What would it look like?) Imagination has a way of kick-starting your clairvoyance. Visit museums, antique shops and second hand stores. These are excellent places to practice.

Some areas that psychometry is useful with are:

> Age of an antique
> Whether a painting is authentic
> If the salesperson is truthful about a product
> Lost or stolen items
> Missing persons
> Crimes or murders
> Personality profile

Psychometry is a psychic tool that is easy and fun to learn. During your unfoldment groups, it will help your gifts open nicely and you will get confirmation of the things you receive.

## Message Work

One of the most popular ways to work with the public now is Message Work. This is very similar to the Spirit Galleries you may see on television by John Edward or Sylvia Browne. Message Work became known in the spiritualist churches as part of the regular service.

Different mediums get up in front of the group or congregation and give short bits of information as evidence of spirit existence. Each message usually is three or four sentences long, with some information the attendee recognizes. This is also known as evidential presentations, platform work or message services.

While teaching Spiritual Awareness Classes as part of unfoldment, I like to include many exercises for the class to practice. Psychometry is used quite a lot, but I also like using direct vibration work. This is using only the connection of personal vibration or voice vibration.

Before starting in the classes, each student was usually already receiving information randomly and without limitation. There had been no instruction on how to present the information and share it with conviction or control.

To practice the direct vibration work, the student stands and is directed to each class member, to present whatever information she receives for them. This is a perfect practice to indoctrinate the student on moving from one person to another quickly, learning to connect and disconnect properly.

When giving short messages or mini readings, it is very important to move from one person to the next without interruption. But just as in the case of the new students, if you have always let the information flow without your direction, you will have a problem disconnecting from one message before starting a new one.

Many of the new students were gifted in receiving impressions and evidence, but had never worked with a mentor or teacher to learn how to present the information. They gave bits and pieces, without structure and did not fully disconnect from the client before moving to the next one.

As a result, more information leaked through for the first client during the second session. They felt compelled to go back to the first client and say what they received. This could be considered disrespectful to the second client.

They were not in control of the presentation, situation or the flow of content. This is where I help them learn the skill of connecting and disconnecting.

Always engage the client at the beginning of the set. Ask permission, or ask for the name of the person you wish to work with. When the name is said, it opens the vibration and aura, allowing you to work with the vibration. Then it is obvious to all you are not intruding.

To completely close the vibration with the first client, you must be firm in the manner you do it. You must be very conscious of your intent and focused the entire time. Be completely in charge.

As you complete the message, look directly at the client, and say "Bless you …Thank you …I leave that with you …or…I'm leaving your vibration." You are instructing your guides that you must move on. Then literally move your body away from the first client and towards the new one.

This technique puts both sides of your mind to work: you must be open to the intuitive side of your mind, but also stay conscious of what you are doing. To work with subtle energies and the spirit realm, you must always be open, but totally in charge, too.

## Preparing the Practice

As I begin a session with a client, I always start with an invocation and protective prayer. I give appreciation to the Universal Creator for being with us.

I ask that ministering angels, teachers and guides be sent to help with information needed at the time. I ask for a pink bubble to be put around each of us.

I believe pink represents love. With love surrounding me, only positive vibrations can penetrate to me. If anything is not positive, the love vibration will purify it. The information is still there, but the harmful vibration is not. It also allows only positive energy to go from us, so no negative thoughts or experiences will move out of our vibrations to harm anyone.

With this prayer said, I am in the mode of spirit. I am tuned in and ready for communication. This is useful for those who give readings for other people, or if you want to connect with information for yourself.

Find the perfect way to protect yourself (and your client) and create a special space to work your ministry.


*Notes* _____

_____

_____

_____

_____

_____

*Notes* _____

_____

_____

_____

_____

_____

_____

_____

_____

_____

_____

_____

_____

_____

_____

_____

# Chapter 7

## *Sensationalism and the Evolution of Spirit Communication*

# Sensationalism and the Evolution of Spirit Communication

I believe the topic of sensationalism is an important one. It helps us see how our thinking about psychics, seers and mystics has gotten to be the way it is. It has evolved over a long time.

After watching society all my life, I've come to this conclusion: The spirituality of mankind has evolved as one giant step in the past 200 years. It has gone from a crude and uncultivated model to more defined and sophisticated.

## Seven Stages

There are seven stages to this giant step of spiritual evolution we as humans have experienced. Going through our lives, year after years, movement seems very slow and uneventful. Even though it seems subtle to many, there are seven distinct areas of change, challenge or growth. These seven stages show how humans have evolved in a definite spiritual manner. We are ready for a huge leap in spirituality.

## STAGE ONE: The Door Opens

The first stage of spiritual evolution started in the early to mid 1800s. In the age of mechanical revolution, many things in society evolved. Life became a little easier.

The Industrial Revolution was a major factor in lifestyle changes. Fashion changed drastically, to accommodate the new lifestyle. The working middle class grew and became stronger. This pushed the upper class of society into a loftier position.

Along with these changes, a deeper desire to find some sense of spiritual awareness became paramount. Religion took on many new directions as well as, esoteric and metaphysical exploration.

People were serious about their quest for spiritual understanding. In the 1800s, Madame Blavatsky formed the Theosophical Society. It was in search of providing knowledge of the spiritual realm.

In 1879, Mary Baker Eddy was instrumental in chartering The Mother Church in Boston. She was founder of the Christian Science Religion and author of *Science and Health*. Another author and researcher, W.J. Colville wrote *A Catechism of Spiritual Philosophy*, besides other books in the late 1800s.

Modern Spirituality

About the same time, the Fox sisters of New York encountered spirit manifestations. There, in the cottage their family moved to in 1847, they witnessed rapping sounds. A deceased peddler who had been murdered in the house was so distraught he needed to make his story known. The Fox sisters had medium-like skills and could facilitate this information.

This was the beginning of Modern Spiritualism and on November 14, 1848, a public meeting was held providing proof the rappings were caused by something other than physical human beings.

The results of the new rapping phenomenon created a widening of communication with the spirit realm.

Mediums, those who are able to receive information through the vibrations of spirit entities started to unfold all over the country.

There was such a stir among people concerning the spirit information. The need for evidence of life after death was very important. Séances became very popular. Mediums gathered with a group of people, and went into a trance-state. There were unknown voices, movement, sounds or some sign the spirit of a loved one was present.

People were more interested in the fact there was evidence of spirit. Because of that, they seemed to lose interest in the concept of spirituality. Evidence of life after death was so interesting. Many people felt the need to continue finding more and experiencing the séance circles as much as possible. In many circles of high society the séance became more of a parlor game.

People recognized what they believed was true: we are not just physical bodies with a mind. But we have a spirit too. Thinking about and considering this idea opened the door for spiritualism. It was very sensational.

Sensationalism of séances and spiritualism started to run wild. Soon it was a popular social event. Mediums were in great demand. It was very lucrative, as well. Imposters began to spring up. To this day, the word séance has many people whispering about charlatans because of its early social beginnings.

People were fascinated with the idea ghosts and spirits visited the earth. Investigations were conducted. Séances became *en vogue*, and socialites entertained their guests with a medium present for spirit manifestation through table tipping or séances.

Andrew Jackson Davis wrote several books dictated through him, by spirit, while being **mesmerized**.

The greatest of these is *Nature's Divine Revelations*. Davis was the founder of the Lyceum, which is the Sunday School of Spiritualism.

Sensationalism: In 1880, Davis became very upset because people were not willing to study the philosophy of spiritualism before they experimented with spiritual manifestation. He said unless people understand the underlying laws of nature, and the philosophy behind spiritualism, they are not helping themselves by using it.

He also believed people were spending too much time in séances looking for so-called miraculous happenings and not enough time growing their soul by the wonderful teaching derived through spirit communication.

The concept Davis was concerned with, seems to be echoed through the years. It forms the basis of my theory of spiritual evolution stemming from sensationalism. This first stage of opening, earmarked a major step by mankind. It took over 200 years to work through the sensational aspect of spirit evidence.

This opening created such a flurry of spirit realm evidence, spiritual camps and churches sprang up all over the country. Several well-known camps still in existence are Lily Dale Spiritualist Camp in New York, Camp Chesterfield in Indiana and Cassadaga Camp in Florida.

These camps were very popular and were hubs of classes, information and spiritual evidence. They created a very strong community of those willing to think outside the box of established religion.

This has created the beginning of a Spiritual Evolution for mankind. It has grown to major proportions, because of our interest and love of humanity.

*STAGE TWO: Introspection*

As the country grew and expanded in different ways, into the 1900s, strife developed in the world. World War I, the Depression and World War II devastated many dimensions of America and her people. Many were stripped down to the bare essentials.

The loss of jobs, finances and security brought introspection and humility. This was how Americans became strong through their pain. We as a people took on a new dimension to spiritual understanding.

There are innumerable stories of destitute men who were hobos in those days, asking for food or shelter in exchange for a day's work. Children wrote letters to Eleanor Roosevelt asking for her family's old clothes to have something to wear to school. Teenagers were unable to pursue higher education since they were needed at home to bring in an extra wage. Homes were lost, families broken.

But humans are resilient. The human spirit and constitution were very strong. Even though the depression left deep scars, the true meaning of community became known.

They had a chance to look at what was truly important and what was not. It gave Americans heart, and an opportunity to hold spiritual knowledge close. Faith took on a new understanding.

Creativity abounded from the spring of humanity. Two of the world's greatest novels were created out of this despair. *To Kill a Mockingbird*, by Harper Lee, and *Grapes of Wrath*, by John Steinbeck, presented painful scenarios of human struggles. Not only from the poor, oppressed or prejudiced, but also a look at those who did the oppressing.

The stories told the truth: How life really was. They gave an honest declaration of recognition. It was as if the authors said, "If we can see and admit the way it really is, then this could be the beginning of making it right."

Truly this was a time of introspection.

The most difficult thing is to look in a mirror and see yourself as you really are. Self-deception was not a luxury to be had during this era. Eleanor Roosevelt has been quoted as saying, "You must do the things you think you cannot do." This time in American history gave the chance to do that.

Since everyone in the country was drastically affected by this state of the union, as well as in other countries, it created a mass consciousness paradigm of thinking that covered the whole world. There was a concentrated area of like thinking so strong it actually brought all of humankind into this spiritual awakening.

*STAGE THREE: Material Awareness and Communication*

The ending of World War II brought servicemen home to start new lives with their families. After such depression, it was obvious the next step would be to re-visit material success. We do live in a physical world, so it is important to put this third dimension into perspective. The third stage of spiritual evolution moved everyone into a perfect understanding of material success and the challenge of using it in a positive way.

American industry expanded, which created growing corporations and jobs. Houses sprouted all over in new suburban areas and a shift in family dynamics created what we now call the baby boom.

The phrase "under God" was added to the pledge of Allegiance to symbolize the importance of family and spiritual values.

Families enjoyed being together. They took vacations together, enjoyed entertainment as a family unit.

Because of the new wealth, automobiles were being built faster, and became a symbol of prestige. Highways were built to accommodate these cars. The middle class became strong again.

The media, through radio, newspapers, magazines and ultimately television, became the most altering tool in the American home. Communication became a huge part of this stage. Radio and television were booming. The whole world suddenly became connected and it opened a dialog with other cultures.

Transcontinental television suddenly linked people of different countries. The arts, including writing and acting, became the most dominant form of communication.

The programs produced on television, of course, never really depicted normal life. However, viewers began to accept what they saw on television as being real. Because of that, Americans began to dream. Possibilities became possible.

We became aware of how other people of the world lived. I still remember *National Geographic Magazine* my parents subscribed to. It was so interesting to read about cultures I knew nothing about. All of a sudden, I felt close to people I did not know. I saw their photos taken by correspondent photographers and saw how differently they lived compared to the way I lived.

This segment of communication, through magazines and newspapers opened us to our neighbors in the world and ultimately, as we will see, became an integral element in the publicity of spirit communication.

*STAGE FOUR: Liberation and Love*

The 1960s revolutionized our way of thinking again. Liberation came to the forefront in many different arenas.

Although liberation brought us legal abortion, it also grounded a revolution of thinking. Everyone, from the President of the United States to school students had an opinion about right-to-life and abortion.

Children and teenagers, who formerly were not included in adult conversations, now became an informed generation. Americans recognized the freedom at hand to express opinions and feelings.

Moral implications began to be addressed, not only about woman's rights and abortion, but also human segregations and an undeclared war in Vietnam.

Love has a way of opening us to understanding. However, truth revealed is sometimes shocking. The time certainly availed us to these shocking truths. The liberating youth of the 1960s seemed to make a break-through in many tension-filled issues.

Looking at the truth, through love, caused an explosion. The young people of America and the world were not afraid to speak out. The communication season of the 1950s evolved into liberation through the youth of the world.

An Opening of Love

Love became the theme of the 1960s: Free love ---unconditional love ---no inhibitions ---cultural diversity. The sexual revolution was beginning, and love was experienced on all levels. Love was opening, even though it was only on a physical level. It spawned a growth in love for humanity that started its blossoming in the 1960s.

The youth of the time pushed that right to the limit, and became the forerunners, spreading love and kindness into the Twenty-First Century.

*STAGE FIVE: Channeled Information and Responsibility*

The next stage of development moved into the 1970s. Spiritual evidence took on a much more serious role in society. Love energies planted on the earth opened to receiving stronger connections with more fully advanced spiritual vibrations.

Those who were unfolding spiritually were doing so in a much milder, but deeper manner. They didn't try to get attention. They only wanted to get information to people who were searching.

This brings us to the difference between "sensational information" and "spiritual information". For instance, the information that got your attention may tell you that your husband had been unfaithful to you, or you should get a divorce.

But information brought about through a spiritual manner will address the reasons you fear your husband is unfaithful, and what could happen if you choose to divorce.

Refined Communication

Instead of mediums introducing deceased loved ones in séances, they were channeling higher-level guides and angels. These higher-level entities are more concerned about humanity and the higher good. As the human majority is evolved, we evolved in spirituality.

The 1970s emerged with channeled information from many different sources. The explosion happened just as suddenly as the séance times of the 1800s. A more refined way of receiving information from spirit was formed.

Instead if going into a dead trance as séance mediums did with
sensational evidence of spirit, channeling was milder. It was a
lighter trance-like state of altered consciousness. Sometimes
channelers were aware of what was happening. Others seemed to
be transported to a lovely scene in the woods and enjoyed the
birds singing while presenting spirit-information.

Mind altering information came from their mouths. A whole new
slant of spiritual understanding was transmitted.

Ring of Truth

Even though the information came in a new and unusual way, it
had a ring of truth. There was an underlying feeling of already
knowing the information. It was more of a validation of
teachings.

One exciting author, Jane Roberts, who became well known in
the 1970s, actually started writing her channeled information in
the late 50s and early 60s. She was always labeled as a writer of
fiction and personal growth.

Those who read her works, such as, *Education of Oversoul
Seven, Dialogues of the Soul and Mortal Self in Time* and *The
Nature of Personal Reality: A Seth Book,* know the books were
written as channeled information from a group entity known as
Seth.

The books she gave us introduced on a large scale the concepts
of reincarnation, out-of-body travel, and exploration of the Inner
Self.

Many other people started channeling to groups of interested
seekers. They started with small groups of friends. It began to
grow as the information of spirituality came into wider
acceptance.

Meditation Spreads

Many jazz performers were open to the teachings of the Hindu religions and other Eastern Philosophies for many years. They quietly practiced meditation, recognizing the expanded understanding of Life.

By the 1970s Transcendental Meditation had come to the United States by Maharishi Mahesh Yogi. This form of meditation became popular because of the interest generated by the Beatles.

These teachings empowered many people to continue their own development. Small meditation groups began to form and people were interested in the spiritual teachings. We were on our way to another stage in evolution.

*STAGE SIX: Healing*

Since the higher energies from the 1970s were coming through the spiritual opening, the energy of mankind started to rise.

The 1980s encouraged the process of this spiritual surge: a higher regard for health, wellness and wholeness became a major concern. This was within the context of health for oneself, others and ecology issues.

A deep impression of brotherly love and concern was generated. Everyone who wanted to help people, whether it was emotionally, physically or spiritually, started to look for alternative and complimentary means to do so.

Out of this desire to help, came many methods of complimentary health: massage therapy, foot reflexology, organic foods/raw foods and nutrition, Reiki Healing/Touch for Health/Touch Therapy, cranial sacral therapy, soul retrieval, emotional release, to mention only a few.

The book, diet for a small planet, written by Frances Moore Lappe', which was written in the early 1970s, opened the minds of many to the possibilities of plant based diets opposed to meat based diets. By the 1980s the idea became much stronger.

Holistic Integration

Physicians also started becoming aware of the body, mind, and spirit connection. Christiane Northrop, who is a medical doctor, became a woman's empowerment physician. She embraced a 'holistic' concept and integrated new, complimentary methods and treatments. Her famous book, *Women's Bodies, Women's Wisdom*, addresses many new ways of honoring the female.

Mona Lisa Schulz is a medical doctor, neuropsychologist, neuroscientist and medical intuitive. Author of *Awakening Intuition: Using Your Mind-Body Network for Insight and Healing*, Dr. Schulz helps us all look at our own intuitive tendencies and how that can help us with our own health.

Dr. Deepak Chopra, author of *Quantum Healing, Perfect Health*, and *Ageless Body, Timeless Mind*, teaches us how to harness the power of awareness. He is known as a physician, healer and spiritual teacher.

*STAGE SEVEN: Full Circle Unfoldment---Media Involvement*

It is time for full unfoldment. As much as we have grown in our spiritual knowledge, there still was a part of us holding onto the tried and true of the past. Sometimes we would rather keep things the way they are. To acknowledge so much, would be to accept major responsibility.

The spiritual surge that took place in the 1800s, especially the time of séances and mediums is closing. It is closing with a big bang.

The spiritual camps and retreats that started in the 19th century had struggled for many years. But in the 1990s they started making a stand again. Many well-known and respected metaphysical speakers and authors were asked to come to these institutions to share their knowledge.

Television Media Sensationalizes Mediumship

Since television has been the most influential aspect of the spiritual movement, networks are now taking advantage of the situation.

I am very aware of how important spirit communication is concerning the after life of our loved ones. Validating they are all right and resolution of relationships are very important to everyone. But this is when television networks saw there was a lucrative side to all this.

The Sci-Fi television network, which is known for its unusual format, took a leap into the spirit world by signing on the Crossing Over with John Edward program. John Edward, of course is known as a very talented medium. However, I feel the programming of this spiritual gift was not shown to its best advantage.

Whenever something is presented in a way to show only one side, it beguiles the viewer into an incomplete picture. This is true of most television programming. (It started back in the 1950s, remember?)

The viewers see only the part the producer wants them to see. As a result, there are three hours of medium work filmed, but about 45 minutes of the session is aired. The *exciting* section of those three hours is what gets on television.

The viewer does not see all the unrelated information coming through. They don't see any counseling provided through spirit. They are only allowed to see the *sensational parts* of the presentation. The medium may have spoken to 2-3 people before he was able to connect with valid spiritual openings.

Mediums are Humans too

This is normal. A medium is only human. Sometimes it is not a good day. Sometimes the spirit loved one is not able to connect through the medium, for whatever reason. Sometimes the participant in the audience is in a bad mood, or doesn't feel well.

There are many reasons why a spirit connection may not take place. But all we see on TV is the connection. Now the general population expects thrilling connections all the time. They were led to believe it happens like that all the time.

It doesn't happen that perfectly every time. Sometimes the most moving information from spirit is very quiet and mild.

This is what the public should be made aware of. This is the kind of information we need: down to earth, honest, "this is how it works" presentations. This is what empowers the population.

True enough, when I am working, I usually read for many people during that time. I usually connect with them on many levels. But no one is always able to connect with a specific person that has passed away and that is not always the most important information.

Shortly after Edward's program started, Tribune Producers introduced a very seasoned medium, James Van Praagh. His program *Beyond*, seemed to take a better direction. James did more counseling through his spirit contacts.

Van Praagh introduced other intuitive methods and personalities so the public would see there was much more to spirit contact than meets the eye.

The problem was the powers to be with that company presented the program during soap opera/talk show prime time. They expected it to become another sensationalized program.

As a result, the producers pushed only the part they thought would be fantastic or exciting. Much of the true information never reached the airways.

In more recent times, programs like *Ghost Whisperer* (created by James Van Praagh), and *Medium*, about true-to-life medium, Allison DeBois, provide a more accurate depiction of spirit communication: Although they are still very theatrical and tend to run the concept into the ground, it is the best television has to offer the public.

There are many new organizations researching and studying subtle energy, and taking a good look at the relationship of the body, mind and spirit, as well as spirit communication.

One organization in particular is the Institute for Noetic Sciences, a nonprofit organization in Northern California. The Institute (IONS) conducts leading-edge research into the powers of consciousness—including perceptions, beliefs, attention, intention, and intuition. It holds open forums and gatherings to inform the community.

The sensationalizing of mediumistic gifts is a hold over from the 1800s. It is now taking its last stand. It has come full circle. Verification of spirit after life is still paramount, but it is time for it to move up a notch. There will always be a place for spirit communication. And the media has brought it to the forefront.

The spirit evolution will be bringing different information. It will be dealing with personal problems in a more inspiring manner. It will not just validate a circumstance, but provide information to solving the problem and counsel to aid in moving through it.

Communion with spirit will become known as a perfect tool for each person to have. Then each of us can have special understanding, connect with universal wisdom and make informed decisions.

Now, the stage is set. The finale: bringing together the physical changes, mental awareness and spiritual awakening of the past six stages---the past 200 years. Finally, the body, mind, spirit are combining to make sense of it.

## Bringing Love into Our Lives

Over the years we have had quite a time bringing love into our lives. The ego has gotten in the way. Society has geared us to be human beings instead of spirits being human; we seem to meet challenges at every corner, just trying to survive in this world. But still, we are searching and growing in our spirituality.

As we look back into the past 200 years, the answer to fulfill our search is much easier than we think. Instead of looking outside of ourselves for validation, the answer has always been inside. Instead of being entertained by sensationalism, we must go further inside to receive the hidden information.

There is a very special connection that will make everything flow easily. It's the go-between I've referred to: Our Spirit, Our Hearts. That is the bridge. That is the "in between" part needing to re-connect the physical with the spiritual aspect of self.

The only way to bridge those two parts of self is to recognize we are truly one with the Universe. We have the wisdom of the universe and we have the love of the universe.

By recognizing the inner self –the spirit-- you can connect with the love the creator intended. It will provide the answers to life. The universe can manifest in you, and through you.

Connect with others of like mind. By joining with others, it gives you the courage to pursue what is important to you.

With the bridge of love working within us, we can choose the perfect path for humanity. With the heart leading the way, your future can only be bright. Only perfection comes through love. There will be no need to look to someone or something else. You will intuitively know the answer.

# Chapter 8

*The Bottom Line*

# The Bottom Line

## *What You Should Expect in a Good Reading*

I would hate to think there are people who just accept what they receive from a reader with no questions asked. So I want to make sure the public as a whole has a good idea of what a good reading is like.

There are things you should expect, as well as things you should not expect. Realize you are the main focus of the reading. It is for you and your highest good.

You should be getting positive and affirming counsel from your reader. It can be a very uplifting experience.

Your reader should be reaching for the highest and best vibrations possible to give a full overview of your situation. Spirit Guides, Teachers and high vibration entities are whom he/she should be contacting.

Connecting with loved ones that passed away is only for confirmation they are all right and sending love. They may assist you by supporting you in your efforts or sending positive energies your way. But they are not sources to help guide you in your life.

If the message coming from the reader just doesn't sound right, you do not have to accept it or believe it. You have the right to say, "No".

But bear in mind, if this is a reputable reader there may be something you need to know about you haven't considered before. Before you say no look at it, analyze the information, or reflect on it later. Things may look clearer to you after the session.

But if the information is way off base, is negative or controlling in nature, back away. This is not an appropriate direction for the reader to take. The reader may be connected with a low energy entity. This could be the way he/she always works, or may not be aware there is other, more positive information for you.

The purpose of a reading session is to enlighten you, lift your spirits and positively inform you of your situation and possible events in the future. You are receiving counsel to make your own decisions. The reader is only there to assist you.

If the reader is bringing you an unknown spirit, do not accept it. The reader may even say, "Maybe you don't recognize him now, but take him home with you."

Please.

If you don't know him, why would you want him in your vibrations? You don't know what kind of energy the entity has and don't know what he wants. Use some caution in this regard.

You should expect to ask questions about the things you want to know. Take some time before you go to the reading to make a checklist. Be sure to take it with you.

Sometimes clients may be nervous about getting a reading and have trouble remembering what they want to discuss. This is only normal. So having the list will keep you focused and in control.

Many readers ask you to make your list ahead of time. This way, information is directed to the universe and is gathered ahead of time to make it easier to access during the reading.

The reader should not be asking you questions. It is a tool often used to lead or fish for information. The only questions coming from a reputable reader will be to make sure you are following the information given. He is making sure you are both on the same page, so to speak.

Expect the reading to take about an hour. Sometimes the information you need may be accessed in twenty minutes. If it is a session with a medium, wanting spirit confirmation of a recent passing, you should be willing to allow more time. The spirit connection does not always happen quickly. Don't rush it.

Also, depending on the type of reading you have, it may require more time. For instance, a full tarot spread will take longer than a short twenty-minute intuitive session.

Expect your reading to answer all your questions. Being told to return week after week is not necessary, unless it is more of a counseling session for a set of particular ongoing problems.

Some readers are upbeat, some are strong and forward in their presentation, some are humorous, others very serious. One is not better than the other, only in the way best for you. If the reader seems too aggressive for your emotional sensitivity, you are not expected to stay. Say so early in the session and make other arrangements for your reading.

You have the right to end a reading if you are not comfortable. But it is only advisable to do so after five-ten minutes, as soon as you realize it. To take up the time and energy of a full reading and then say you don't think it's a good match is not good etiquette.

It is a complete waste of your time and the reader's energy. In fact, the reader may even suggest the reading is not proceeding in a good way, and suggest you reschedule, or even see another reader, depending on what is happening.

I am the first to recognize if I am not getting a good connection, or the session just doesn't feel right. I will either ask for another scheduled time, or offer the names of different readers that fit better with the style or substance needed for the client.

Once in awhile, the client really doesn't have any specific questions, but wants a general reading. I may suggest they go to a tarot reader or palmist I know, for the type of session they want.

Sometimes the reader is not connecting with the loved one you request. In fact, sometimes, if a client is so intent on speaking with only one special spirit, it might not happen at all. Spirit is not always conducive to pressure. As much as you may want it, and as much as the spirit loved one may want it, does not mean it will always happen.

Each reader has his/her own style. Do not expect all readers to have the same manner in presentation. If unsure, always ask ahead of time how the reader works. He should be happy to give a short explanation of how he proceeds in a reading.

For example: if asked how my readings proceed, I say, "I always start with a prayer of protection and invocation. I share information I receive from my guiding forces at the start of the session. Then I open it up for you to ask specific questions. I work with your spirit vibrations, my spirit guides, and include Earth Cards as a small portion of the reading."

If you are getting a palm reading, you must expect the reader will hold your hand at least part of the time.

If you have an aversion to being touched by a stranger, then palm readings may not be your cup of tea.

A tarot reader will be able to give you a full reading by using a spread of cards. You may not have to ask questions during this session, but I always feel it is important to do so. Then you are sure to get to the source of your interest.

Astrology readings will be different. There usually is a section of the session requiring the reader to calculate your specific information.

As you can see, there are many types of readings and many types of readers. So be flexible as to what to expect. However, the reason for the reading is for your betterment and to provide information for you to make life decisions. This is always the main purpose a reader has for your session. The reader will help you find the source of concerns or challenges and give possibilities to strive for, or change for positive life growth.

After having a good psychic reading of any type, you should feel empowered and good about the choices you are making and directions you are moving in your life.

## Suggestions for Consulting a Psychic or Medium

Recognize it takes two people to have a reading. It is your obligation to be "present". You need to be sure of what you want. What questions are you going to ask? What direction do you want the reading to go? Be attentive and open. Listen to the information given.

Make sure you book your appointment when you can prepare yourself ahead of time. This helps you feel unrushed. Make time after the reading to reflect and take it all in.

As the client, you are the one wanting assistance. Be sure the reader understands the direction you want the reading to go. Always be open-minded to the possibilities presented. Of course, it is your choice what to do with the information, but being open to something you may not have considered will empower you, during your decisions.

Consider these points:

- Do you need a medium or psychic? A medium offers communication from spirit energies and the higher realms; a psychic attunes to and interprets the energy field from the sitter.

- More money doesn't necessarily mean better information.

- No medium can promise communication from particular spirit loved ones. Conditions must be right. If you are grieving because of a very recent loss, this may not be the best time to consult a reader. You could be influenced by the need to contact your loved one.

- Whatever you have planned for the future is listed in the spirit realm. The energy of the plan is in your aura and can be accessed; but you have control of the outcome. Plans can be changed.

- Maintain your own power. Spirit loved-ones wish to communicate to let you know they are OK, that there is life after death. Then, to support and inspire. Those loved-ones should not tell you about career, romance, and finances. That is not their job. It is not their place to tell you how to live or what decisions to make.

- This applies to readers, too. Do not give away your power to another person.

- Know when to stop. Just as there is addiction to alcohol and gambling, consulting a reader can cause dependency and obsession. If a reader is suggesting you come back weekly, there is something else going on. There could not possibly be more to cover in a week's time.

A good reading can be a very beneficial thing and should assist you through any concerns in your life and possible future endeavors. It should cover at least a six- month period, if not a year.

If you are dealing with a special problem, such as grief or a developing situation, you may require several sessions. This would certainly be considered a spiritual counseling rather than mediumistic communication with a departed loved one.

## Psychics Can Have Bad Days

There can be no real guarantee when it comes to communication or psychic connections. Everyone has down days. This goes for readers as well. It has nothing to do with their abilities. It just doesn't always happen. Many factors fit together to create a connection. If one small bit doesn't fit the puzzle perfectly, it can interfere with your session.

A truthful reader will admit it to you, and suggest rescheduling the appointment. The only one with the power or ability to affect any change you are wanting in your life is you alone.

Getting counsel from a reader is always a good thing, but for informational purposes. No reader can make someone fall in love with you or solve any problems for you. But they can give you invaluable information and inspiration to assist you in your quest.

## *Determine if a Reader is Right for You*

There are many quality and professional readers for you to choose from. But knowing ahead of time how the psychic proceeds in the reading is important. You want to have a competent and honest reader. There are simple guidelines for this process:

1.  Know what you want. Why are you going to a reader? Is there something specific you want to know? Is it about a past problem or emotional issue? Do you want to see what is possible for the future? Is it dealing with the loss of a loved one? What is the bottom line?

    It is easier to interview your potential readers knowing what information you want. Find out if their focus and style fit your needs. Quite often, any type of reading can work with a life question. It is the reader's psychic ability, or skill with divination tools, that supplies your answers.

2.  You are shopping for a life consultant. Your interview should reflect that desire. Ask questions to find out exactly what you want to know about them: How long have you been a reader? Who were your teachers or mentors? What are your thoughts about giving readings? How do you receive your information and what kind of things could you tell me? What is a typical reading like?

3.  Ask if he provides a taped reading. If not let him know you will be bringing your own recorder. It is important for you to refer to and receive full benefit of the reading.

4.  How do you feel while talking to the readers? Do they answer your questions to your satisfaction? Do they take the time to explain their answers fully? Expect the same results in the reading.

## How to Be a Good Reader

Over the years, I have taken the time to assess the manner in which I give readings. When appropriate, I adjust or make changes to the presentation. The areas I have listed below are common sense things I would appreciate, if I was getting a reading (or interaction with anyone for that matter).

- *Make Sure the Client is Open to the Information*

Set up a proper understanding with your spiritual guides and higher self for only appropriate information to come through. Advanced readers know intuitively how much information should be given to a client. All clients may not be at the same level of understanding in spiritual areas. Be aware to these differences in your presentation.

- *Use Your Own Style of Spiritual Connecting Prayer/Protection*

Before starting a reading, always go to your spiritual center and say a brief prayer asking for permission on a higher level and for all communication coming from the connection is truthful, forthright and accurate; and the interpretation is true. Intend the communication be for the highest good of the client and something important to the client be revealed in the session.

- *Correctly Give the Information You Receive*

There are appropriate ways of giving information you get from your guides. Do not try to change it or try to make it fit. It may be understood later. Present it in empowering ways, so the client can benefit from the information and not be fearful. If you sense a warning of some kind, also ask your source for follow through information to assist your client to a proper completion.

If you are receiving symbols, be sure to tell them the actual symbol, since it may mean something to them literally. But always include your interpretation of the symbol. (See Symbols in the Chapter "The Unfoldment Process") Honor however he may interpret it. But it is given to you by the connection you have with your guide and it should be shared as your understanding of that symbol.

- *Understand How to Access the Highest Energies Possible*

In your training or studies, you learn how to connect with the most beneficial and finer vibrational energies possible. Bringing in a loved one from the other side is not enough. This is only mundane information and although reassuring to the client, it is only a small part of any good reading. Practice sending love out from your heart and see it reaching into other loving realms for the best information available.

If you get negative information or fear-based connections, this is not appropriate for your client. Work at raising your personal vibrations. Take an honest and hard look at who your guides are. Make changes if need be.

- *Discern the Spirit or Vibration*

By this time in your career (and after reading this guide), you should know what kind of vibrations you are working with. Sometimes entities disguise themselves to play pranks or adversely influence you. If you are in the least bit skeptical about your sources or do not feel comfortable with them, demand they leave you. Then do whatever you can to raise your vibrations.

- *Read With Love*

Always read from a place of love. This is where the foundation of your spiritual lifestyle is important.

If a client asks for a reading and you have just had a difficult time in your personal life, you will need to recognize whether it is appropriate for you to enter into a reading consultation. Or you may need to spend a certain amount of meditative time before the session to clear yourself. You want to always bring the best vibration to your clients.

- *Know When to Stop*

Some clients will be enraptured with the whole medium-oriented concept and want multiple readings too close together. Don't let ego guide you. Information doesn't change that rapidly. Suggest a longer distance between readings so you will be able to serve them properly.

- *Set the Tone of the Reading*

Know your worth, and be worthy of your knowing. But more than that, know when you read easily and how to space your sessions. Maybe you are fresher in the morning. Make that time for your appointments.

Know when the reading is complete and graciously end it. Some clients try to pull more information from you and actually rob you of energy. They may or may not be aware of doing it. But you should be aware of it ahead of time and know how to close your session and your energy field.

- *Continue Your Studies and Practice*

Learn your trade over a period of time, with a teacher or mentor you have trusted for many years. Do not stop learning. The more you stay fresh and up-to-date with your trade, you will feel confident and your clients will appreciate you.

## *Suggestions for Becoming a Reader of Integrity*

1. Always encourage your client to think for himself.

2. Never discuss the consultations you give with others.

3. Only give insightful and meaningful information.

4. Only give readings to someone who has asked for one. By plunging into an unsolicited reading or passing conversation with personal information you are barging into someone's space unannounced and probably unwanted. This is considered bad taste and invasion of privacy. The spirit entity giving you this disrespectful information is of a very low level and should not be encouraged.

5. It is inappropriate to "read over" another psychic's readings. If a person asks you to tell them what another psychic meant, be very gracious, but suggest the person return to the psychic and ask for clarification. Remind them it is their option to ask for clarification at the time it happens. Also, make sure your clients understand what you are giving at the time it is given.

6. Unless you have extensive studies and training in medical intuition, stay away from it. Only licensed medical doctors can give medical advice, so don't put yourself in a bad situation. You are dealing with a real person's life. If you do receive information concerning a health issue, suggest your client goes to his health care practitioner. Let it be known you do not diagnose or prescribe for their health issues. (Check out more information I have in the Chapter on "Intuition, Psychics and Mediums".)

7. Inform your client know no matter what information comes through, they can take active steps to change it if needed.

8. Whenever you are personally close to a situation or client during the reading, you run the risk of getting caught up in the emotion of it. This is never helpful. It enlists sensationalism I speak of in this text, and will most assuredly get attention. But you end up missing information from the source because you are too involved in the situation instead of maintaining control of the reading. When you lose control, you are apt to let in lower entities. Your reading will become useless.

9. Know when not to give a session. When it becomes apparent to many people you are a psychic, they may ask you for information anytime of the day or night, expecting you to tune in at their will. Don't fall for this. It does not empower you. It opens you to being used.

10. Finally, if you are having a bad day, or need the extra cash, or feel pressured to perform as a psychic or medium, think twice. It is not the environment you need to conduct a positive and uplifting session. Adjust the appointment when things are better suited for it.

## *What a Faked Reading Looks Like*

There are many opportunities for someone to fake a reading. Sometimes it occurs because of the client's unfamiliarity of what to expect and demand in a reading. A dishonest person can take advantage of this opportunity. Other times the reader in question uses parlor tricks to create a reading atmosphere. They may not even believe in psychics, but use this as a scam just to get your money.

If you are very new at grieving the loss of a loved one, now is not a good time to look for a medium. You are still feeling raw and not in full capacity of reasoning.

These are times unethical readers can take advantage of you. You want certain information, and no matter how unethical a reader is, you will only see the information through the eyes of loss and pain. Wait until you have moved through many of the varied stages of grief.

The main way to fake a reading is to give what is called a cold reading. This is done by playing off clues the client gives unconsciously, or by paying attention to details about the client's appearance or actions.

*SIDE COMMENT: Cold Reading is the ability to manipulate you into thinking the expert knows something about you. Experts of this deception watch what you do and say, and closely observe your clothing and slight idiosyncrasies. These things help him lead into telling you half truths, or generalizations. He will watch your response and glean more information. These are faked readings and do not have anything to do with true psychics or mediums.*

For instance, the reader may nonchalantly notice a few stray cat hairs clinging to the sweater of the client, and with his eyes closed, say something like, "I'm seeing a cat in your vibrations that is very close to you, and has been trying to send you a telepathic message."

Of course, the client will be delighted to acknowledge it, and may even tell the reader the name of her cat! This gives more information to work with, since the names of our pets quite often reveal the appearance or attitude of the animal.

The fairly new television program called The Mentalist really opens the door to see what tools can be used by fakers while trying to make you think they are giving you a real psychic reading.

Some expert mentalists consistently observe the client: noticing body language and the manner in which she/he is dressed. The expert may start out with stating general terms to see what kind of reaction he gets from the client.

He pays attention to skin color changes, body movement, and the eyes (if you look up or down, side to side, or even the dilation of the pupil). This way he can assess the attachment to the statement, or catch something to hone in on.

By recognizing what attracts the client, the expert knows what direction to take the session. Even if the information is incorrect four times and correct only once, the one time is what the client will remember or hang on to. This is called selective thinking: we all do it. And the expert capitalizes on it.

We usually believe what we want to, no matter what else may be happening. If you go to a reading and the reader is very off base, it won't matter. If you really want to believe he is good, you will experience it that way. This is what mentalist experts rely on.

The irony is not all cold reading techniques are done by dishonest people. There are many untrained or un-mentored readers (psychics or mediums) who unknowingly work with cold reading techniques.

It seems normal to them; it works; people are astounded, so they continue, thinking they are mediums. They really don't have any way to measure their technique with anyone else, so they believe their talents are spiritual gifts.

Another form of this deception is "fishing" for information. The expert could start the reading with a very vague bit of information. "There is a female presence around you from spirit."

If the client hasn't already responded with a name of someone she wants to visit her, the expert says, "There seems to be the name with a letter S…Susan, or Shelley…" He looks for a response. The client may say, "You mean Sarah?"

"Yes, of course, that's what she's saying…Sarah. Sarah is here sending her love to you." This is a combination of fishing for information and then leading the client to a conclusion.

Then, my personal favorite way of recognizing a faked reading: asking the client for the answer. "Do you have a mother is spirit?"

"Yes! She is."

"Yes, I see her very close to you. Did she die of something in the chest area? The lungs? The heart?"

"Yes, she had a heart attack."

"Yes, I know, she tells me it was her heart…a heart attack."

This has always frustrated me when a reader asks questions instead of stating what he sees or hears. To be absolutely clear the reader is true with the information, he should be telling you instead of asking you: "I feel a mother around you in spirit. She seems to have passed away with a condition in the chest area…either the lungs or heart…I am not clear on that point, but know it was the chest area." This way, we (both the reader and the client) know there was no fakery in the presentation of information.

Then ask if that makes sense to the reader. If it doesn't, then the reader knows he is in the wrong vibration, or getting the wrong information, and can re-direct his connection.

Now, there are plenty of readers who are true with their connections and information, but have always asked the client instead of telling what they have. There are several very well known mediums that do that. It's just the way they have always done it.

Personally, I always make a point of telling it the way I see it. I may even bend over backwards to get the information out, but I never ask my clients questions until I have stated the facts as they come to me. Then and only then, I'll ask for confirmation, not fish for information to feed back to the client.

This is why I stress so strongly the reader should never ask questions referring to what he might see. But state as a matter of fact what he sees, then ask if it is something the sitter recognizes. If it is not, then that's fine. But there was no fishing involved. And the sitter will be sure of it.

*Question:*
*If you are a medium, is it right to charge for your services? After all, it's a gift from God, isn't it? It seems like you are cashing-in on God's goodness by taking money for it.*

*Answer:*
*I love that question and I grappled with it for many years myself. A friend and associate medium when we were mainly working within the Spiritualist Church got a small booth at area psychic fairs and charged money for sample readings. I was aghast! To my understanding she was defaming the spiritual gift by charging for readings.*

*Several years later, I went to a psychic fair just to see what it was all about. Besides readers and vendors, there were several people giving lectures about different spiritual and metaphysical things I was interested in. The attendees were hungry for information. They did not know about spiritualism, but still were interested in finding out about such things. The sample readings done there helped the public understand what spirit communication and psychic abilities were all about. I looked at it differently after that.*

*Let me ask you this: Have you ever bought a beautiful painting because the artwork and colors were so special? Have you ever had your transmission rebuilt by an expert mechanic who had been recommended to you? Have you eaten at a five star restaurant and tasted the exploding flavors of the Chef's specialty? Or bought an engaging musical recording by an aspiring songwriter/singer?*

*All these people have God given talents, as well. Would you suggest these artists just give you what they do, without any kind of compensation? If you'll notice, the artists and chefs and mechanics that are extremely talented and sought after receive the highest pay. Being a medium, psychic or intuitive is no different.*

*Many readers have been led to do this spiritual work full time. It is their ministry. Ministers from many religions get a salary, and earn their living that way. Do not judge anyone who is asking for payment as an even exchange of energy.*

## Final Thoughts

The best way to become a reader with integrity is to build a foundation by finding out who you really are. Spend time studying various forms of meditation, spiritual growth and the higher understanding of mankind and of being spirit.

We are realizing we are all go-betweens, existing here in the third dimension and there in the spiritual dimension: trapped in the physical body. Now it is our goal to learn how to operate in this manner and know we are spiritual, blending our energies in the secular. Recognize you are the centralized component; the center; the heart of the matter; in between.

Begin to work with your own symbols that represent parts of your life. That leads you to the information you need in making decisions for yourself. Begin to connect with your friends, neighbors and strangers on a soul level. The light you grow, you can see in others.

Use the exercises outlined in this book to strengthen your intuitive skills, the meditation methods to raise your vibrations, and the ethical information to bring about a pride and honor in the world.

Whether you are an aspiring psychic, seasoned medium, or you are looking for one, realize you are the only one who can really know truth—your own truth. If information is given to you intuitively or by a reader, look at how it feels to you. Do not accept it on face value. Know if it rests in your heart well.

Always strive to be the best you can be at whatever endeavor you move towards. Always give your best to others.

Whenever you seek advice or guidance from any professional, know some are ethical and some are not. By using awareness, careful consideration and the information found in this guidebook, you can find honest, caring and gifted guidance.

*A Declaration of Integrity:*

1. *I have studied and developed my spiritual gifts to the best of my ability. I will give you the names of my teachers, mentors and peers I studied with.*

2. *I will always be honest with the information I receive, or not receive.*

3. *I will explain ahead of time, how I work with Spirit and how the reading will proceed.*

4. *If after several attempts I am not able to contact to your loved one, I will tell you and suggest we try another time.*

5. *I will never barge into your energy field without your permission. To do so would be an invasion of privacy: no less than breaking into your house and searching through your private belongings.*

6. *I will continue to study and hone my craft so I will always be able to assist you on your path.*

7. *I will not ask you leading questions and then feed your information back to you.*

8. *I will always bring a positive and healing energy while working with you.*

9. *I will always strive to connect with the highest spiritual energies available.*

10. *I will not lie to you or try to persuade you into any particular way of thinking.*

11. *Predicting someone's time of death can actually affect the outcome. I will not take part in it.*

# Glossary

**Akasha Repository**
Akasha is an energetic place in the Mental Plane where the distilled knowledge of the universe is stored. It holds the records generated of everything that happens in the universe as it occurs.

**Apports**
Objects, such as stones or flowers materialize and are transported out of thin air into the séance room: physical mediumship.

**Astral dimension**
The astral is the next stage of awareness after the physical body dies. The spirits of those who have passed away inhabit the astral on their path to full transition. The astral blends the physical and etheric planes.

**Astrology**
Astrology is the study of heavenly bodies using the positions of the planets, stars and moon, to learn what influences they may have on human life.

**Aura**
The emanation of energy surrounding the physical body and attaches the spirit to the personal body.

**Automatic Writing**
Automatic Writing is the process of receiving written communication from spirit or Higher Self without conscious control. Some call it channeled writing.

**Body Mind Spirit**
In addition to the physical body we have a mental and spiritual body. A combination of all three makes you whole. The word holistic comes from that understanding.

## Channeling
To channel is being in a very light stage of trance to communicate information in a narrative form, such lectures or classes.

## Clairvoyance (Clear Vision)
Clairvoyance is seeing visions in your inner psychic eye, also called the Third Eye.

## Clairaudience (Clear Hearing)
Clairaudience is hearing words, phrases, or music in your head without physical means.

## Clairsentience (Clear Sensing)
Clairsentience is sensing or knowing something: also called empathy and psychic knowing.

## Control
Control is the sharing of mental and physical energies between the medium and spirit. By allowing the spirit to take control of the medium, phenomenon can happen.

## Direct voice
Direct voice is brought about by spirit entities who speak in a séance without the use of a physical body.

## Divination
The art of foretelling the future is finding the lost and finding solutions to everyday problems by being open to vibrational knowing.

## Ectoplasm
While a medium is in deep trance, the spirit entity links and gathers etheric energy (ectoplasm) to create physical manifestation.

**Entities**
Spirit beings of those who have lived in physical bodies, or have never had physical form.

**ESP**
Extra sensory perception is receiving information or knowledge of an event before it occurs.

**In spirit**
To prepare one self to commune with spirit energies: Moving away from the outside world.

**Intuitive**
To look within: Being aware of outside information by receiving it as a hunch or gut feeling, sometimes unconsciously.

**Medical Intuitive**
A medical intuitive is a person who is sensitive to and reads the vibration of another's health condition.

**Mediumship (mental or physical)**
Being aware of the vibrations of spirit beings and receiving information from them.

**Mesmerize**
To be in a hypnotic or trance/channel state, first popularized by a man named Mesmer.

**Metaphysical**
The understanding of things other than physical; includes body, mind and spirit studies.

**Numerology**
Numerology is an ancient study, understanding the science and vibration of numbers as a divination tool.

**Palmistry**
Art of telling fortunes from the lines, patterns and marks on the palms of the hands

**Paranormal**
Phenomena beyond the normal experience or understanding of an ordinary man

**Pick up**
Being able to receive information by tuning into certain vibrations

**Precognition**
Knowing about a future event without foreknowledge

**Psychic**
A person who connects with the energies of a person or place to receive useful information

**Psychometry**
Holding an object (keys or watch) and receiving information in the form of impressions or visions through its energy vibrations

**Psycho-Navigation**
A spiritual journey done by shamans: The soul of animals enter their souls to teach them things, after trance state is accomplished

**Reading (reader)**
A planned session, in which a psychic or medium receives information about a person or event.

**Reincarnation**
After dying, the spirit is able to come back to earth in another body to experience another lifetime

**Spirit guides**
Guiding forces from the spirit world or Higher Self that assist each person in their lives

**Tarot**
An ancient art and science using a special card deck to divine information.

**Telepathy**
Mental connection relaying information from one person or spirit to the other

**Trance**
A medium goes under control by a spirit entity to receive evidence of life after death. Usually used by physical mediums.

**UltraSense(TM)**
Having the use of extended senses by using the five senses to an enhanced degree to perceive spirit dimensions

**Unfoldment**
Taking the time to grow communication with spirit or develop psychic gifts.

# References/ Other Resources

Gallup Poll, Committee for the Scientific Investigation of Claims of the Paranormal in 2006, http://www.gallup.com

*Three Magic Words*, U.S. Andersen. 1954.
ISBN 0-87980-165-4

Edgar Cayce,
http://www.caycelibrary.com

Jane Roberts, Seth Material.
http://www.sethlearningcenter.org

*The Secret Doctrine*, Madam Blavatsky. 1888.
http://www.secretdoctrine.net   ISBN 978-1585427086

*The Holy Bible*, King James Version

*Awakening Intuition*, Mona Lisa Schulz. 1998,
ISBN 0-517-70758-6

*Ageless Body, Timeless Mind*, Deepak Chopra MD. 1993,
ISBN 0-517-59257-6

*The Oversoul Seven Trilogy*, Jane Roberts. 1995,
ISBN 1-878424-17-3

*Excellence: Can We Be Equal and Excellent Too?* John Gardner.
1961, ISBN 0393018482

Harry Price Library of Magical Literature, University of London
http://www.shl.lon.ac.ul/specialcollections/hpl.shtml

American Board of Scientific Medical Intuition,
http://www.ABSMI.com

*You Can Heal Your Life*, Louise Hay. 1999
ISBN 1-57170-628-0

*The Book on Mediums*, Allan Kardec. 1874
ISBN 0-87728-382-6

Theosophical Society in America,
http://www.Theosophical.org

Integrating Science and Spirituality, Lee Bladon
http://wwwesotericscience.org

Lesson in Theosophy and Planes of Existence
http://www.users.ez2.net/nick29/theosophy

The Secrets of Creation, Reality Creator Books
http://www.wisdomsdoor.com

Institute of Noetic Sciences (IONS)
http://www.noetic.org

Lily Dale Spiritualist Camp, Cassadega, New York
http://www.lilydaleassembly.com

Camp Chesterfield Spiritualist Camp, Chesterfield, Indiana
http://www.campchesterfield.net

Cassadega Spiritualist Camp, Cassadega, Florida
http://www.cassadega.org

Akashic Records/Akashic Energy, Tammi Rager
http://www.wyndravin.com

Omega Institute, Rhinebeck, New York
http://www.eomega.com

*PsychoNavigation, Techniques for Travel Beyond Time*,
John Perkins. 1990   ISBN 0-89281-300-8

*Extra Resources* _____

_____

_____

_____

_____

_____

_____

_____

_____

_____

_____

_____

# About the Author

Rev. Melissa Leath is a Metaphysician, *Life!* Visionary and Spiritual Educator and has been a Certified Spiritual Medium since 1982. She was ordained as a minister in 1996, through The Circle of Light and Love Church, in Springfield, Ohio. Melissa has extensive training as a metaphysical counselor and has given private intuitive-spiritual counseling to thousands of clients.

Rev. Leath has taught many personal empowerment workshops and classes in basic meditation, new beginnings, spirit communication, spiritual symbols of the subconscious, emotional and physical healing techniques and intuition. She and her husband, Charles, who is a reflexologist, travel extensively, providing workshops and private sessions.

Melissa writes for DreamWeaver Magazine (http://www.dw-magazine.net) and is the author of *The G0-BETWEEN: Bridging the Gap* (which was the forerunner to this book); *Meditation, Plain and Simple Workbook* and *Outrageous Living: Tips & Secrets to Thriving in the 21st Century*. She put together her own guided meditation CD *Soul of the Universe*, as well as other lectures, e-books and audio programs.

Melissa is the director of The Orange Blossom Center for Enrichment, which is dedicated to the teaching and better understanding of basic meditation, inner strength and personal peace, within the family and world community.

She is quickly becoming recognized as expert in meditation and spiritual growth and affectionately known as Meditation Maven.

Melissa and Charles offer many lectures, workshops and intensives:

- Emotional Release: The Heart Path
- Spirit Code: The Language of Spirit (Personal Symbols)
- Basic Meditation
- Metaphysical Tools of Empowerment
- Multi-Dimensional Awareness
- Intuition, Psychic Abilities, Mediumship and UltraSense
- Reflexology for Personal Use

Other resources provided by Rev. Leath are her websites:

www.123SpiritualGrowth.com
www.MeditationWarehouse.com
www.MeditationMadeEasy.com
www.OutrageousLiving.net
www.PsychicIntegrity.com

## Jeremy Simmons, Graphic Artist

Simmons is a professional graphic and web designer. He has been creating artwork – as he puts it – "since I was old enough to deface the walls of my home and now it only seems right that I continue to add my graffiti to the world's canvas."

You may reach him on his websites:
www.jeremynet.net
www.fourtowersdesign.net
www.dungeonartist.com

## John Ford, Photographer

Having been a medical photographer, John has served as instructor of Biomedical Photography at Ohio Institute pf Photography & Technology. He is an honorable Fellow in the Biological Photographic Association and now retired, enjoys Nature Photography and Photomicrography.

He can be reached by email:
jfordbpa@yahoo.com

Many thanks to Jeremy Simmons and John Ford for their talents in creating the book design for Psychic Integrity cover.

*Notes* _____

_____

_____

_____

_____

_____

_____

_____

_____

_____

_____

_____

_____

_____

_____

_____

3750355

Made in the USA